THE ROUGHSHOOTER'S DOG

MICHAEL BRANDER

THE ROUGHSHOOTER'S DOG

· THE ·
SPORTSMAN'S
PRESS
LONDON

This edition © Michael Brander 1989
Originally published 1957: 1958 and later revised
This edition published in 1989 by The Sportsman's Press

British Library Cataloguing in Publication Data
Brander, Michael, 1924–
    The roughshooter's dog – New ed.
    1. Gun dogs for rough shooting. Training – Manuals
I. Title
636.7′52

ISBN 0–948253–38–X

Printed in Great Britain by
Redwood Burn Limited, Trowbridge, Wiltshire

CONTENTS

	Foreword	7
1	Introduction	9
2	On Training	19
3	Primary Obedience	31
4	First Stages in Retrieving and Steadiness	45
5	On Scent and Scenting, Gamefinding, Pointing and Flushing	59
6	Advanced Training	79
7	Brace Work and Trials	90
8	General Remarks on the Use of the Dogs and Training	99
9	A Full Bag	112
10	A Blank Day	123
11	A Day's Partridge Shooting	131
12	A Day's Pheasant Shooting	141
13	Wildfowling	151
14	Two's Company	163
15	Extracts from a Training Diary	170
16	Diary of an Ex-Policewoman	181
17	Postword. Mainly on the G.S.P.	194
	Glossary of Technical Terms	198

ILLUSTRATIONS

Keeping position at halt with lead. *facing page* 32

Keeping position at heel on lead. 32

The long drop to raised hand and blank. 33

Early dummy retrieve. 64

Initial retrieving – ignoring temptation. 64

Learning to drop to rolled dummy. 65

Dizzying pigeon. *between pages* 80–81

Bringing youngster on point under control.

Early lesson in flushing game. Dizzied pigeon.

Point on fur – hind leg raised.

The point may be made with head high or low.

Game flushed, the youngster drops and marks fall.

Lesson in steadiness.

Advanced training. *facing page* 96

Steady on point. 97

Honouring flush. Dropping to flushed game. 97

A hare is pointed. 128

Flushed and shot. 128

Retrieved. 129

Youngster honours point of older dog by
  backing. *facing page* 160

Early water retrieve. 160

Contrast in styles 161

Brace work on river bank. Pheasant held. 168

Duck and pheasant shot. 169

Foreword

SHORTLY after this book was first published in 1958 the Kennel Club in Britain recognised Field Trials for 'those breeds which hunt, point and retrieve'. These Field Trials are run with the dogs working singly in front of at least two guns and two independent judges, but otherwise differ little from the 'Meat Dog Trials' mentioned on pages 96 and 97. This recognition by the Kennel Club has been the only real change since this book was written. In the meantime however the number of owners of pointer-retriever breeds has very greatly increased, both in this country and overseas, notably in Australia and New Zealand. More and more people have come to experience the tremendous satisfaction of training their own rough-shooting dog. Yet few professional handlers are prepared to train the pointer-retriever breeds, since the time required to establish the necessary harmony between handler and dog in all the varied aspects of their work together is too great to make it economically worthwhile. "The understanding between a good working general purpose dog and his trainer is not achieved in a few weeks, or even months, indeed it often takes years to achieve and many people only achieve it once in a lifetime, if at all. It should be the aim of all who own a pointer-retriever to achieve this harmony between dog and man or something close to it. This book is intended to provide a guide

7

towards that goal. It can be nothing more than a guide, since dog and man should be learning from each other throughout their respective lifetimes and each combination is different, but at least it should serve to help the novice who otherwise does not know where to begin."

In 1983 I was commissioned by Pelham Books to write an entirely new approach entitled *Training the Pointer-Retriever Gundog*, including chapters on Brace Training and Field Trials. The only twelve lines the two books have in common are those above in quotation marks. The two books are indeed complementary to each other providing between them some forty years distilled experience of working pointer-retrievers. Popular demand for *The Roughshooter's Dog* has certainly remained high and I still meet people who claim to have trained field trial champions or just good sound working pointer-retrievers with it. I am glad to say that I still feel the same enthusiasm for working pointer-retrievers that is apparent in its pages. I dedicate it . . .

To
MAX
Werra & Freddy

My very grateful thanks and acknowledgements are due to Alex Brown for the illustrations.

ONE

Introduction

OVER THE centuries man and his dog have hunted together and, though the shotgun and rifle have replaced the bow and the spear, few of the basic methods of hunting have altered. Even in modern shooting today some of the old hunting cries still survive. In roughshooting the old methods of working with a dog are basically unchanged.

In order to be sure of his sport the roughshooter requires a dog. Such a dog must be more than merely a retriever ready at heel to fetch the game which his master has shot, although that must be a part of his duties. He must also be able to range ahead, quartering the ground and finding and holding the game. It is as a gamefinder that the dog must excel.

Of course there is nothing particularly new or startling about this. Many roughshooters have always used their dogs in this fashion, and before the days of game rearing on a large scale most shooting dogs were expected to work thus as general purpose gamefinders and retrievers. All the same there are undoubtedly a large number of people to whom shooting over dogs is a novel experience.

Nevertheless, as it becomes accepted that, due to modern farming methods and lack of keepering, the old days have passed irrevocably when game could simply be walked up and bustled from underfoot by a spaniel, so the rough-

shooter must learn to adapt himself if he is to shoot anything at all. To this end he must train his dog on general
purpose lines for the sort of work he is going to require
from it. Here, however, is precisely the point at which the
person not accustomed to this type of dog work is liable to
stick. Before going any further, therefore, it is advisable to
start by indicating what is required from the roughshooter's dog so that the meaning of the term general
purpose dog may be clearly defined.

The roughshooter's dog should be able to range wide or
close according to the nature of the ground and his
handler's signals. He should be able to find game and,
once found, he should ideally come on point and hold it
until his handler arrives within range and he receives the
order to flush. He should also be able to find dead or
wounded game and retrieve it to hand. He should be able
to work in water, in cover, or the open with equal facility.
Such a dog must be a combination of pointer (i.e. air
scenter) and retriever (i.e. foot scenter) and is therefore
best defined as a variable-range, variable-pace, Pointer-
Retriever.

At first sight this seems to be expecting a great deal, but
on reflection it will be realised that for years the slow and
steady short-range Pointer-Retriever has been known to
us in the varied breeds of the spaniel. Furthermore most
of us at one time or another have known the labrador or
retriever that would point, and equally many have heard
or know of the pointer that would retrieve. There is
nothing particularly out of the way in the idea. It may be
argued that the spaniel is essentially pointing foot scent.
This admittedly may sometimes be the case, but at other
times is equally certainly not so.

Most people will agree that in practice any dog which
is worked in front of the gun as a gamefinder, even when
kept in well within gunshot, soon begins to distinguish

between air scents and foot scents. Watch the retriever
trained to work the ground slowly and methodically
within gunshot. As he catches an air scent his tail starts to
move and he advances showing interest. A moment later
and the game is flushed. With a little more training he
could have been taught to hold steady in a staunch point.
On the other hand take the picture of a pointer working
out the scent of a covey of partridges that have been
flushed. Then the air scenter is clearly following a foot
scent. It will generally be admitted therefore that any
dog which has learned to hunt for game must also have
learned scent discrimination, or the ability to differentiate
between air and foot scent, in the process, even if it has
not been trained to point.

There are those who argue that no dog is ever taught
to point, but that it is purely instinctive. There is also the
school of thought which maintains that the pointing
instinct has been produced by clever and discriminating
breeding from dogs which showed the natural pause
before springing on their prey to be seen in the behaviour
of the wild fox. A similar school of thought maintains that
the retrieving instinct has been developed from the natural
instinct to carry prey back to the den. Since even terriers
and mongrels will fetch sticks and balls and sometimes
point after a fashion these theories seem to have a sound
basis in fact. There is certainly no doubt that the wild fox,
or dog, will often scent the air standing still with the head
held high and will also follow a foot scent with the head
down. The logical conclusion is that both the instinct to
point (air scenting) and to retrieve (foot scenting) are latent
in most sporting breeds. Training a dog to point is therefore merely a matter of encouraging instinct to develop
fully.

Admittedly it is obviously true that pointers, whose
instincts have been developed in this direction by breeding

and use for generations, will tend to point more readily than retrievers. Conversely retrievers will probably retrieve more readily than pointers, but in either case the other basic instinct should still be latent and it should always be possible to develop both together. With patience instinct can usually be encouraged to develop and almost any breed with instinct enough to hunt for game can probably be trained both to point and retrieve.

It is, however, perfectly true that some dogs cannot be taught to point, just as others cannot be taught to retrieve. As everyone knows, some breeds of gundog have been bred for show-looks to the extent that there is scarcely any of their original working instinct or ability left in them. Quite apart from instinct, the dog that has been bred purely for show-looks usually hasn't a single brain left in its head either, and almost everyone will agree that there is more to sound game finding and good gundog work than mere instinct. To be successful the dog must have brains as well as instinct and use them in conjunction with its handler.

The well trained retriever that will work far out in front of his handler in response to hand signals and whistle to effect a retrieve has much in common with the pointer which works to hand signals and whistle in front of his handler. It is this conjunction of brains and developed instinct and the ability to work at a distance in harmony with his handler which makes the general purpose dog, and the training is not much more complex than that of the specialist gundog if it is approached methodically on sound lines.

There is little doubt that the aspect of training the general-purpose dog where most people go wrong is in not allowing them to range freely. Unfortunately all matters of range must be largely dependent on individual estimates. There are people who invariably take their shots at twenty yards and think they are at forty or more. It is difficult to convince them otherwise. Similarly I have heard people talk airily of ranging pointers half a mile or more across a moor, whereas, even supposing the ground made this feasible, I cannot feel that this could have been the best method of using them, for to get the best out of any dog the handler should be within reasonable controlling distance.

The average person to start with, however, has an instinctive fear that if the dog is ranged out of gunshot game may be flushed and lost to the bag. So many people have seen an untrained dog run in front of the line and flush game out of gunshot that it has become second nature to restrain their dogs and keep them in to heel, or at most to curb their ranging well within gunshot. But even if some game is lost in this manner before the dog has settled down to being a staunch pointer, it must always be remembered that probably that game would not have been found had the roughshooter been walking up in the ordinary way with his dog at heel or ranging close at hand. It is well worth bearing with any such initial mistakes and persevering until there is complete confidence and understanding between dog and handler and the dog has become a reliable gamefinder.

Of course not all dogs can be expected to achieve perfection and, as always, in the field some dogs will be much better and more reliable than others. Similarly some handlers will expect their dogs to do more than others and other handlers will be satisfied with less. Some dogs will work fast, others slowly. Some will point staunchly and rigidly, others will merely stand with tail gently moving. Some handlers will not object if their dog runs in to the fall when game is shot; in certain circumstances, more especially abroad, in a different terrain and climate, it may even be advisable to train them to do so.

More probably the handler will wish his dog to remain steady until ordered to retrieve.

Much must depend on what is required, on the ground, on the handler and on the dog. All that can be done in any book is to indicate certain elastic principles which can and must be applied differently in each case. If sufficient working instinct is there to start with and if sufficient time and trouble is taken over his training, the intelligent and suitably built dog of almost any gundog breed taken steadily along the lines indicated should develop into a sound roughshooter's dog.

For the past few generations opinion in this country has been against the use of dogs in this general purpose fashion. Instead the accent has rather been concentrated on further and increased specialisation of each breed for one particular task. "The Jack of All Trades is Master of None", has been the cry and such prejudices die hard even when circumstances have altered. During the heyday of shooting in this country, prior to the first world war, it might have been reasonable to keep a kennel full of specialist dogs. However, the gradual eclipse of some of the specialist breeds, such as Clumbers, except for show, or as pets, is a pointer to the end of a period. Few people nowadays can afford to keep two or more specialist dogs. The trend is back towards the early days of the shot gun when the pointer was expected to retrieve and above all he was a gamefinder.

Partly because the spaniel suited our needs hitherto, and partly because of this prejudice against the general purpose dog, from which even the spaniel suffered not so long ago, there has been little interest in breeding a general purpose dog in this country. It is probably for this reason as much as any other that many roughshooters can look back on a useful general purpose dog which they have owned or known, which was virtually a mongrel.

The crossbred dog, as has often been noted, frequently shows surprising intelligence and adaptability. On the other hand, there is little incentive to breed from such a dog for there is no likelihood or guarantee that its progeny will be of a similar stamp.

On the continent however, especially in Germany, where game has usually been scarcer, there has always been a greater interest in perfecting a general purpose dog. The German Short-haired Pointer, the Weimaraner, the Poodle-Pointer, the Hungarian Pointer and many other general purpose breeds have been developed and have found their way to this country and further afield; notably to the U.S.A. where the idea of a general purpose dog has been popular for a long time.

The often misused term "dual purpose" in this connection is misleading, if only because you can obviously use a Pointer-Retriever in three ways. As a pointer alone, as a retriever alone, or more correctly in its general purpose role as a Pointer-Retriever. As applied to any general purpose Pointer-Retrievers the term "dual purpose" merely means that they both point and retrieve. The description general purpose, or multi-purpose, is more exact, but, as has already been shown, even this requires qualification. The description "Dual purpose: Showbench and Working" used by some kennels is an illustration of the need for exact definition.

Paradoxically it is comparatively easy to go wrong in training one of these general purpose breeds. The average owner, seeing how highly developed his dog's instincts are, feels that it must be a comparatively simple matter to train him and only finds out too late that there was more to it than he had expected. This in itself demonstrates the importance of knowing at all times exactly what you are aiming to teach your dog to do.

Even a dog of a general purpose breed cannot be

expected to work properly unless he is correctly trained. If he is kept consistently in to heel like a specialist retriever his initiative will naturally be curbed. Equally if he is consistently ranged far out he will be tiresome to bring in to heel and he will work badly close at hand. In his training as in his work, for the first few seasons at least, the general purpose dog should be kept constantly on the alert by changes of work and scene as far as possible.

Although the way each individual works his dog must vary according to the ground and the handler himself it is clearly a bad principle always to work the dog over the same ground in the same way. To get the best out of his dog the roughshooter should give him as much variety as possible and more especially so during training. Too much of any particular type of work to the exclusion of others is liable to cramp all-round ability.

Nor, it must be stressed, can perfection be expected at once, or even in a short while. The work that the general purpose dog is expected to perform, if he is to do it efficiently, is more complex than that of the specialist dog. Correspondingly the training must be expected to take longer. Even with a general purpose breed there is more to training than simply taking the dog out with the gun. Too often I have heard the same fatal words:

"I just took him out with the gun and he worked perfectly."

Of course this is usually far from true. It is merely another indication of the different standards different handlers may require. These owners are forgetting in the thrill of their occasional triumphs the many occasions when things have not gone perfectly. Yet with a little more time and trouble spent in training they might have saved themselves many disappointments.

Admittedly in the training of a general purpose dog, even more so than in specialist training, it is impossible to lay down any hard and fast rules. The majority of training methods I have suggested are easily applicable to a dog of a general purpose breed and there should be few failures with them, although there are always occasional duds in any breed. However it is always worth persevering with a suitable dog, even if at first no headway seems to be made, and, in course of time, at least a working measure of success should be achieved.

No definite time limits or schedules can be laid down in any methods of training, but more especially in training a general purpose dog. For example most strains of Springer are natural retrievers as soon as they are weaned, but it is usually the second season before they start to point naturally. Yet some may well vary in this, and there may even be the exceptions which naturally point first. It is always unwise to be dogmatic about such an uncertain and variable matter as dog training. With a crossbred dog especially it is hard to say how it can be expected to develop, and the trainer must simply take each dog as he finds it and vary his training to suit the dog.

Some schools of thought favour teaching no retrieving in the first season as they maintain that otherwise there is a risk of the dog not remaining staunch on point. In practice, while I entirely agree that pointing and retrieving should be kept absolutely separate in the dog's mind to start with, I do not feel that it is a wise plan to stifle instinct. However, as far as possible, whenever I have been aware of any such theories I have done my best to mention them and explain my reasons for either agreeing or disagreeing with them as fully as possible.

Inevitably much of what I have to say will be old stuff to many people, but there are always others who are new to the idea of roughshooting with a dog, or to training a general purpose dog, or for that matter to training any gundog. It is primarily for them that this book is intended,

B

but many owners of general purpose dogs may find it useful to have their ideas put into concrete form and some of the suggestions put forward may be new to them.

The main point that I hope will be well driven home is that in order to achieve a really useful general purpose dog it is well worth while taking a good deal of time and trouble over the training. Even if one season's sport is curtailed and some chances are missed that might otherwise have been taken, it should be worth it many times over in the sport that is finally gained and in purely personal satisfaction when the game is found, pointed, flushed and retrieved perfectly by the dog you have trained yourself.

TWO

On Training

BEFORE GOING on to actual methods of training there are a number of general points worthwhile making. Firstly it should be stressed that it is desirable, if possible, for the owner to train his dog himself, because in the thorough training of a dog, as with a horse, or indeed any animal, a very special relatiohship should be formed between the trainer and the animal. By this I do not mean that the animal should be dominated or in any way cowed by the trainer, but rather that it should of its own free will co-operate fully with him and enjoy doing so. Once this desirable state of affairs has been fully achieved, and it will not be achieved either easily or quickly, no one else will be likely to get the same results from the animal in question. Nor to my mind is it possible to assess this relationship in terms of money, and it is almost a breach of trust to sever it. Anyone who has had to part with an animal in which this highly personal relationship has been achieved will understand what I mean.

It is almost impossible to do more than generalise in any question that involves people and animals and it is dangerous to try. Just as some people have natural hands and sympathy with horses, while others, however hard they try, remain wooden and mediocre, so some people are naturally good with dogs and others are incapable of understanding them and training them effectively. Then again there are many people who simply have not the time to spare and rather than spoil good material such people should send their dogs away to be trained by a competent trainer.

Human nature being what it is, of course, most people are too vain to think that this can apply to them and those sufficiently obstinate will probably first make a thorough mess of the job and spoil the dog for subsequent handling. Fortunately, however, there are more people possessed of the gift of sympathy with animals than might be imagined. People are often not even aware that they possess this gift and regrettably some are not even interested. If the owner is honest with himself, he should soon know to which class he belongs and, if he has not the time, the patience, or the temperament to train the dog himself, then it is infinitely desirable that he hand the job on to someone else who understands what he is about.

From this it will be appreciated that I strongly advocate the training of the dog by the ultimate handler if at all possible, and it is for the handler who has never trained a general purpose Pointer-Retriever, or come to that any type of gundog, that I am principally writing. It is at this stage that I would like to stress a point that is all too often overlooked, especially by people training their first dog. Each dog is as different from the next as chalk from cheese. Therefore, though certain training methods may be suggested for guidance, they are for guidance pure and simple and in each case may be applied differently. The important thing is that the trainer should know what he is trying to train his dog to do and have his ultimate aims clear in his own mind. To this end certain methods of training may be indicated and occasionally alternatives given, but basically there are only two things that count. One is the dog, the other is the handler.

With a good dog it is possible to take steps that would

mean ruination with another. Similarly a trainer with understanding and patience can do things that another, without the same sympathy and understanding of the canine mind, should never even attempt. It is important here that blind love and sympathy should not be confused. Blind love of animals, by itself, can lead to more harmful handling than wilful neglect. There are few things more repulsive than the overfed, disobedient, spoiled dog waddling ahead of its proud owner, who is probably under the impression that all is well with his, or her, little darling and would be greatly offended to be told otherwise.

It is up to the would-be trainer therefore to examine and assess his own capabilities first and then those of his dog. Apart from the question of instinct, there are some dogs, like some humans, who are slow to learn a lesson. Others will be quick to learn without repeated tuition. It cannot be too often emphasised that dogs have widely differing personalities like human beings and every trainer must make a study of the temperament of a puppy before starting its training. It is obvious that a nervous dog requires more careful handling than its more robust kennel mate and so on. Thus in a way the professional trainer is faced with a more intricate problem than the psychologist when he takes on a new dog. He must study its temperament and its reactions and judge from them how much of its misbehaviour is due to wilfulness or high spirits and how much to mishandling by the owner. To a skilful trainer it soon becomes an easy matter to judge, in spite of the fact that his charges cannot speak. In matters such as this actions often speak louder than words.

But instinct plays a very large part in the gundog's training, especially a Pointer-Retriever, and it is clearly not worth the professional trainer's while to attempt to train pups that are deficient in natural instinct or that have been mishandled. In the former case the training is

likely to take too long and in the latter case a cure can
never be certain and there is always the likelihood that, on
returning to the owner who has mishandled him, the dog
will simply revert at once, representing so much wasted
labour and probable blame for bad training.

Though it is fashionable to write about the psychology
of animals as if it was something that had been newly
discovered, most animal trainers worthy of the name have
long accepted it as a matter of course that animals may
react in certain ways to training. These reactions, or
resistances, mostly have simple and appropriate counters
by which training can be carried on effectively. While I
am suggesting various methods of training I will also do
my best to mention the most common of these resistances
that the amateur trainer is likely to encounter and the
most likely methods of dealing with them.

Of course, to begin with, for proper training it is really
essential that the pup should be kept in a kennel away
from distracting influences, so that it looks forward to
its daily exercise and training with keenness and interest.
A dog kept in the house will inevitably be subject to
influences which will tend to distract it and undermine
correct discipline. Since many owners will want to keep
their dog in the house and train it at home and since it is
the object of this book to try and help them to do so, I will
however indicate the important points to remember.

From the moment the pup arrives, be it kept in a
kennel or the house, all commands used must be clear
beyond doubt to both owner and pup. There must never
be any confusion of commands. The same command for
the same action must always be used. By distinct repetition of each command with no danger of confusion of
words in the dog's mind, the training is at once simplified.
The words themselves do not matter as long as the same
distinct short sound is always used for the same command.

Repetition of tone of voice is probably more of a help to begin with than many people realise and any gestures associated with commands should be used from the start and, like the command, always repeated in the same fashion for the same command.

Instances of these points might well be given. Never on any account give confused commands such as, "Come away, come here to heel." "Heel" in such circumstances is all that is required and far more effective. If a gesture is being used such as patting the knee, then it must always accompany the words.

It is always important, however, to make sure that the dog's attention is fully gained before giving any command. Here is where the value of a short clear name for the dog is demonstrated. The dog's name may be called, or a short whistle given, purely to attract the dog's attention to the command which is to follow. Anyone who has been in the Services will appreciate the value and necessity of the cautionary word of command (i.e. "Squad" or "Company") prior to the real order. The attention of the ranks is drawn to the fact that a command is coming. They are ready for it when it comes. There is no danger of catching them unawares or of them failing to hear it. So it should always be with handler and dog.

Anyone who has been in the Services will also appreciate how words of command may degenerate into mere sounds, i.e. "Order Arms" becomes "Awdah Hype." Yet they are none the less effective for their vocal transformation. In fact in many ways they are improved. The very ring of them is enough to cause the ranks to move as one. The effect with animals is just the same. So long as certain simple, separate and distinct sounds are associated with certain meanings, that is all that is required. To carry this one stage further and have certain clear and obvious gestures as well as certain sounds conveying certain meanings to the dog is not to tax it unduly, so long as progress is made at the dog's own pace.

This question of when the training should start and at what pace it should continue is one where it is possible to go very badly wrong. It must be appreciated that although limited training should start from the moment the pup is weaned it is important not to overdo it. Many good dogs have been spoiled by starting intensive training too young. At the same time all dogs, like all humans, should be learning something every day if possible. In many ways the more gradual this process is the better, but to my mind it should start at once and continue to the last. The importance of encouraging instinct and channelling it into the right lines cannot be overstressed, but again complete distinctions must be drawn between individual dogs.

It has already been pointed out that some dogs may be completely devoid of what one would imagine to be instinctive reactions. Some dogs develop late and others develop early. It is impossible and dangerous to generalise. The only thing that can be stated flatly is that each trainer must judge from his estimate of the dog's capabilities and his own when to start serious training and at what speed to go ahead. If he is at all doubtful, the slower the better is probably the best answer. On no account should training ever be hurried.

It is a great danger that the overkeen amateur trainer may force the pace too fast for the dog. This is akin to over-training and the results are much the same. If the dog is forced ahead too fast during training it begins to make mistakes. It sits down when it should be quartering, or refuses to come when called. If on the other hand over much training with the dummy or similar work is given once the dog is fully trained, the results can be as bad. The dog will stop and mouth the dummy or shake it, or simply refuse to retrieve it at all. A dog suffering from either of these all too common faults lacks keenness and interest.

It is always vital in all phases of training that the dog's interest and keenness should be maintained. If it shows any signs of being bored or its interest begins to slacken, then it is time to stop lessons for the moment. Better by far that several short lessons should be given than that one should be protracted too long. In this connection, while it is always important to get a dog or a horse to perform a lesson well, it is often better to stop at once rather than force the issue and risk defeat. Rather change the subject and get some other more simple lesson performed perfectly, such as coming to heel and sitting, then the next day pick up the lesson again. This time it is probable it will be performed successfully without trouble. In this as in many other instances animals are like children. It is almost always easier to lead than to drive, although there is always the exception that responds only to being driven.

Whether the dog develops early or late, it is not suggested that his training is by any means completed when he first takes the field in earnest. On the contrary that is probably when the real training begins. For it is in their first season's serious shooting that most dogs are made or spoiled and even a good dog can always be spoiled by injudicious handling, however well it may have been trained previously.

It must therefore be obvious that any attempt to lay down any definite time for training or to say definitely that a dog may be trained in such and such a time is tantamount to an impossibility. Even when a dog has been fully trained by a professional trainer and returned to its owner, it cannot be said to be more than on the threshold of its fuller education in the field.

Although the system of training I suggest is aimed at

keeping the dog in ignorance of the killing power of the gun and the more obvious pitfalls of field work until it is already steady and reliable, I must make it clear that the only way a dog can learn ultimately is in the field. The more work the dog gets once its basic training is over, the better gundog it is likely to be, providing always that its work is supervised correctly. If this is done there is no reason why the owner should not have a dog of Field Trial standard. In practice, however, the average owner is not interested in Field Trials. He is happy if his dog does what is expected from it without glaring errors.

So long as the training is being carried out on the right lines there is very little effort involved in seeing that your dog does not commit the more obvious offences, and it must always be borne in mind that prevention is better and easier than cure. A word from you at the right moment will stop your dog from transgressing. Therefore don't be afraid to act quickly and raise your voice if necessary. Next time you may not even need to warn him, but if you once start to let the dog get away with it the rot has begun to set in. It is always important in training and in practice to keep one jump ahead of your dog mentally and observe likely temptations and forestall them before they arise.

It must be remembered that the general purpose Pointer-Retriever is even more of a partner in the business of shooting than the specialist dog and a careful line must be drawn between allowing him too much freedom and curbing his initiative. In training therefore it is always important to distinguish between disobedience and simple lack of understanding on the dog's part. As the training becomes more advanced it is sometimes difficult to be certain that the dog has understood the orders. In any such case of uncertainty it is almost always better to give the dog the benefit of the doubt rather than risk the possibility of sowing the seeds of uncertainty in the dog's mind. Better by far to repeat the circumstances carefully again, making certain that the mistake is not repeated, rather than punish the dog for what may have been your error of judgement.

The bad old days of animal breaking rather than training are now happily past. It is hardly necessary for me to condemn the practice of using spiked collars and similar training methods. If you cannot do without them you had better have no part in training a dog. Similarly the continual use of the whip is a confession of failure. Correction may certainly be necessary at times in some cases and when it is should be applied promptly and effectively. Excessive use of the whip, however, can only result in a spoiled dog and a frustrated owner. The dog will never be reliable since it is always balancing punishment against transgression and sometimes the scales will tip in favour of transgression. It is perfectly feasible and in fact desirable to train a dog without resort to physical punishment at all.

It is in this connection that a solemn warning must be given. If you do decide that you must punish your dog, do, whatever happens, make sure that punishment and offence are certainly related in his mind. It is no use, for instance, calling a dog to you for running in and then beating him. This is a common mistake and will simply lead to the dog refusing to come when called for fear of a thrashing. Punishment must always be instantaneous with commission of the offence. If the dog runs in then put him on a check cord and give him the opportunity of repeating the attempt. Then really bowl him off his feet. It is unlikely he will need a repetition.

At one time or another I have heard it suggested that either a catapult, a light air gun, or cartridges loaded with salt should be used to punish a dog at a distance on the instant commission of an offence (e.g. running in). To me this savours of the last resort and I am frankly dubious of the cures claimed in this way. It might conceivably be all right once with an old offender if you could guarantee to place your shot correctly without danger of injury to the dog, but better not attempt it if you can't. It is better by far not to allow matters to reach the stage where such punishment is required and, needless to say, such methods should never be applied to the young dog.

Certainly on no account should a shotgun ever be turned on a dog. This extraordinarily foolish practice is asking for a balled cartridge and a dead dog and it is probably better off dead than remaining with an owner who behaves in this way. Even if it does no more than pepper the dog it is still liable to make him gunshy. Apart from that there is the very real danger of blinding him or otherwise wounding him seriously. Anyone who does this, whatever the provocation, should never be allowed to keep a dog. In fact any man who cannot control his temper would be well advised to leave the training of dogs to others, for he will never get satisfactory results.

In actual practice it must always be remembered that, however heinous a dog's offence may seem to be, the handler is probably at least partially to blame. We do not blame a car for running down a steep hill when we forget to put on the brakes. Similarly, if a dog misbehaves, then the handler's standard of control is probably to blame somewhere. It may simply be that the dog is off colour, or has not been sufficiently exercised, or that in some other way the handler or trainer has been at fault. In any case, it is better to aim at preventing any recurrence of the error than simply to lambast the dog. Better by far to give the dog a chance to repeat its error and check it sharply, nipping the offence in the bud, than to administer a pointless thrashing.

Most puppies while full of life and vitality are quite easily cowed. Of course the younger they are, the more this is the case. Very little punishment should be required. A stern 'No' is probably more than sufficient in most instances. If the high degree of personal relationship between handler and dog, which I advocated, is to be achieved this must obviously be so.

It should be accepted that utility is the keynote of all efficient training and every order and action should always be examined with this in mind. In general any order or action which does not serve a genuine purpose should be dispensed with entirely. In this connection it will be noted by the reader that I advocate the teaching of the command 'Sit' but make no mention of any other command to drop. From a purely utilitarian standpoint it matters not the slightest whether the dog sits or lies. If you wish to teach it the difference by all means do so. I do not advocate it as I consider it is liable to confuse the puppy.

As I see it, the fewer the commands and the greater their scope, the easier it is for the dog and the trainer. Once the dog is efficiently trained any number of frills may be added that you wish. It is never too late to learn for dog or human and the trainer should always be trying to perfect the understanding between himself and the dog. The more he can project his wishes to the dog and the fewer commands he has to give, the higher degree of training he has attained.

In all matters of training the trainer must remember that if he sets a high standard for the dog he automatically sets a similar high standard for himself. It is worth repeating that clarity, consistency and incisiveness of command at all times are essential and the trainer must always be clear in his own mind what he wants his dog to do. Yet once the dog is fully trained and working well in the field in unison with his trainer, it is again up to his trainer to remember that now he is probably the less efficient half of the partnership. It is often wisest then to leave matters to the dog to work out for himself. In any case, each time out, both trainer and dog should be learning something fresh, even if it is only that they are still not perfect.

THREE

Primary Obedience

IN THE introductory chapter on training I have already indicated that the owner should train his own dog if possible. Many people do not do so because they are under the impression that a great deal of special equipment and carefully prepared grounds are necessary, whereas nothing could be further from the truth. Apart from an occasional assistant, a blank pistol, some easily constructed dummies and a length of stout cord, very little out of the ordinary is required. Almost any open space will do to start with, so long as it is reasonably free from distracting influences and some degree of privacy can be assured. A small paddock or field will do perfectly.

While it does not do to start the full training too soon, it must be understood that once the puppy has become accustomed to its new surroundings and to the trainer there are certain simple points of primary obedience it should learn. It is important however that the trainer should gain the puppy's confidence from the start. If any difficulty is found in doing so, a few choice titbits as an approach to its heart the nearest way, through the stomach, will be certain to succeed. In the initial lessons also a few pieces of biscuit may be used as a reward for work well done or a lesson well learned and they do help to stimulate interest and attention. The trainer must beware of overdoing this however and causing the puppy to look for a titbit as the accompaniment of lessons.

Nothing is more tiresome than the dog that is constantly looking for a titbit at each move of the trainer's hand.

To begin with, the lessons must be kept short and the standard of obedience expected must not be too high. For, until the puppy understands fully what is required of him, he will naturally be awkward and it is vitally important at this early stage that, even if the puppy transgresses, nothing should be done to make it feel that it has been punished for obeying. It is very easy to sour a pup at the start. More than ever at this stage patience and quiet repetition without loss of interest are the keys to success.

It should never, for instance, be necessary to shout at a puppy. Firmness of tone should never be confused with bellowing. It is, indeed, sometimes advisable to give commands in a low tone deliberately to exercise the puppy's hearing and enforce attention. It is a fact that dogs that are constantly shouted at become immune to it and are unlikely to obey commands given in normal tones. If the puppy has irritated the trainer by some piece of disobedience, either deliberate or accidental, it is not advisable to do anything other than return the puppy to its kennel and continue the lesson the next day. All lessons must be taught with a cool mind and no suggestion of temper or hastiness. The puppy will quickly sense any such atmosphere and very soon lose faith in its trainer.

One last caution before going further. Many people, especially those training their first dog, use far too many words of command. The aim must always be to use as few as possible and to be able to use signals to convey them if desired. Clearly this is worthwhile as it is aiming at increasing the understanding between dog and trainer. The more redundant words of command, such as 'Come here', 'Stay' and so on, that are used, the more difficult it

Keeping position at halt with lead.

Keeping position at heel on lead. The puppy is led so that it has no option but to keep position.

The long drop to raised hand and blank.

is for the dog to understand what is desired even though it may well be easier for the trainer.

There are many different ideas and definitions of primary obedience, but to my mind, once the puppy has learned the meaning of the commands 'Kennel' or 'Basket' and 'No', it consists of teaching the dog to walk to heel, to come to heel from a distance at command, whistle or signal, to drop at command whistle, signal or shot, and to stay put at command or signal. This may sound a great deal to learn to begin with, but when it is considered that this is all covered by the two commands 'Heel' and 'Sit' and by the signals of hand patting knee or thigh for 'Heel', and a raised hand and a stamp of the foot for 'Sit', it will be realised that it is not in fact too much to expect. In practice, taken properly through the training, the average puppy can absorb it easily and quickly. The importance of it can scarcely be overstressed however, since, once the puppy is over this primary training, it is half way to being a trained gun-dog.

Taken together then, these are the aims of the primary obedience training and, to a certain degree, they should be taught as one lesson. But the degree of intensiveness with which they are taught must clearly vary with the puppy's degree of mental and physical development. Obviously a three-to-six month old puppy must be taken more gently than a six-to-nine month old puppy. In the former case two to three months might well be taken over this initial training if necessary, whereas in the latter case a month or even less might suffice. To try to teach a young puppy too intensively is to court disaster and will almost certainly result in a ruined dog.

To begin with, if kept in a kennel, the command 'Kennel' must be understood. If kept in the house it is even more important that a distinct corner of its own with its basket must be understood when the command

C

'Basket' is given. This command is very easily taught by placing the puppy gently in the required place while repeating the command in firm tones. Very little repetition will be found to be needed before the command is understood perfectly.

Any attempt at evading this command may be greeted with the word 'No' and a repetition of the command. As a prohibition of any action not desired, 'No' is also quickly understood and is the more necessary in the case of a puppy kept in the house. Undue and unnecessary use of these restrictions, however, like the word 'Don't' with children, can easily lead to a cowed and broken-spirited or soured and mutinous youngster.

Used sparingly and on suitable occasions, these are the first steps in primary obedience training and are very easily taught and understood. There are two other aids to this initial training which should never be overlooked. One is the puppy's tendency to run towards its kennel or basket and the other is its eagerness for its food. Both these instinctive reactions should be utilised to the full.

Taking it for granted, then, that the puppy has learned the meaning of the commands 'Kennel' or 'Basket' and 'No', and has learned to trust and like its trainer, the training for primary obedience, as I see it, starts very simply with the trainer entering the kennel and putting the puppy on the lead. He must then lead it to the spot where it is intended to start training. If necessary, to begin with, this may only be from the basket to the centre of the room. The lead is held while walking so that the puppy must walk to heel and the command 'Heel' is reiterated once or twice to impress the point should the puppy attempt to stray.

The point being reached where it is desired that the lesson should take place the trainer halts, stamps his foot and says 'Sit' firmly. The pup is then gently but firmly pushed into a sitting position, still 'at heel' as would be the case later on. That may well be enough for the first lesson.

The next stage of the same lesson is that the trainer turns round, still holding the lead without strain, and faces the pup. Holding his hand up palm outwards he should then take a step backwards, at the same time repeating firmly the command 'Sit'. It is probable that the pup will try to move. A firm 'No' must then be rapped and the command 'Sit' repeated. If necessary, the puppy is pushed gently back in a sitting position. The trainer may then turn round and continue the walk, puppy at heel, until he feels the time is ripe to repeat the lesson.

For the first few days repetition of time, place and inflexion of voice all help to impress the lesson on the puppy's mind. It is worth emphasising once again at risk of being tedious that undue sternness of voice or inflexion with a young puppy may be sufficient to sour it. The puppy should at all times, as far as is compatible with discipline, enjoy its lessons.

It is at this point that I advocate making the puppy 'Sit' before it is allowed its meal. The plate of food being held above it and the command 'Sit' being given, a ready obedience is likely to be obtained. The reward for obedience being considerable in the puppy's eyes it will be the more instantly obeyed.

At feeding times, therefore, the drill will be to call the puppy from its basket or kennel to 'Heel' accompanied by a pat of the hand on the knee. Once in the heel position, the command 'Sit' follows at once and this will quickly become automatic. The next stage is the introduction of the command 'No' when the food is placed on the ground within reach of the puppy. The puppy is restrained from moving from its position and the command

'Sit' may be repeated with accompanying stamp of the foot. After a moment or two the fingers may be snapped with a wave towards the plate and the puppy may be allowed to eat. The length of time the puppy is kept in a sitting position may then gradually be lengthened until a full minute or more elapses.

This training with its use of the stamped foot may be carried on concurrently with the other method already mentioned, using the raised hand towards the puppy. In this way very soon the trainer will be able to take the puppy out on the lead in the heel position and halt, while the puppy sits automatically, then turn and walk backwards several paces away from the puppy, hand upheld and ready to repeat a warning 'No' or the command 'Sit' should the puppy attempt to move.

A stout length of cord should be added to the lead at this stage, unknown to the puppy, and the trainer, placing himself between the puppy and the kennel, may now add the command 'Heel', dropping his hand and patting his knee, or thigh, invitingly. Should the puppy not come instantly, or attempt to stray, a jerk on the cord will suffice to make up his mind. On coming voluntarily and well, he may then be made much of and rewarded with a titbit. Make sure, however, that he returns to the correct heel position.

The next stage of the lesson is calling the puppy with command or signal alternately and dropping him, by means of the command 'Sit' rapped out clearly and upraised hand, when he is half way towards the trainer. The puppy should obey instantly by this time and should then be called to heel and rewarded. Should he fail to sit, when told, he must be firmly placed in position and the performance repeated.

This may continue with the trainer gradually in-creasing the distance between himself and the puppy until eventually the lead and cord may be dispensed with and the lesson can be repeated free. Should the puppy then disobey, however, the command 'Sit' must be rapped out, the checkcord replaced and an opportunity permitted for a repetition of the disobedience. Should the puppy then disobey again, a sharp tug on the check cord should be sufficient to convince it that transgression is not worth while.

In actual practice the trainer will find that so long as this training is carried out in conjunction with the feeding training suggested already, the puppy should soon be sufficiently advanced for the trainer to walk out with it at heel, halt and leave the puppy sitting with a stamp of the foot and walk out of sight, without the puppy trying to follow. In fact, he will soon be able to leave the room or kennel with the puppy sitting in front of its food and return with the perfect assurance that the puppy will not have moved.

It is advisable, naturally, to choose some position for this training where the puppy can be left so that it is visible to the trainer but not the trainer to it. If the puppy then shows any sign of movement the trainer can restrain it by word of command. On the other hand the training should be nicely graded so that no strain is put on the puppy and the advance each day is well within its powers.

When walking away from the puppy the trainer should walk straight away, or the tendency otherwise is for the puppy to follow him round with its eyes, pivoting slowly on the spot, rather than staying absolutely still. Properly taught, this lesson is one of the most important of basic steadiness.

At this point the whistle may be introduced. I personally believe in having two distinct whistles, one with a high pitch, such as is produced by the so-called silent whistle, and the other a more piercing and distinct pitch. The former is first introduced in conjunction with the hand patting the knee so that the puppy soon connects it with coming to 'Heel' and will answer to it alone. The latter is used at first in conjunction with the upraised hand as the signal to drop, and after a very short space of time the puppy will connect it with the command and respond by dropping to it alone.

It is possible for this purpose to use one of the specially manufactured two-tone whistles such as are used by shepherds. It really does not matter what is used so long as they are quite separate and distinct and each is only used for the purpose that has been chosen for it. Needless to say, the puppy must never be confused by needless blowing, or by blowing of the wrong whistle. One long blast on either should be quite sufficient for practical purposes.

Later on it may be convenient to use the call whistle, as opposed to the drop whistle, for short blasts to attract the dog's attention when it has ranged too far and a change of direction is desired. In practice a sharp whistle through pursed lips will probably suffice as well for this purpose, but in any case it must be appreciated that this comes into practice much later. At this stage of training great care must be taken not to confuse the puppy, and indiscriminate whistling at any time is a very bad thing for both dog and handler. As with verbal commands or signals, every whistle blast should have a meaning and a purpose which must be obeyed or it is so much waste of breath and time.

Once these lessons have developed partially along the lines suggested and the puppy can be guaranteed to drop to stamp of foot, upraised hand, or whistle, the firing of a blank pistol may be introduced. The puppy should have been tested for gun shyness very early on by clapping the hands together smartly, but in any case it should now be accustomed to the sound gradually by firing the first blank behind the back when the puppy is some distance away. If there is no sign of fear the next blank may be fired with upraised hand, causing the puppy to drop automatically. In this way, in a very short time with surprisingly little repetition required, the first steps in the all important lesson of dropping to shot may be well and truly brought home. The puppy soon associates the stamp of the foot, the upraised hand, the whistle and the sound of the blank as well as the command with the one action. The all-important point to remember is that once thus dropped the puppy must never be allowed to move without further orders.

Once the puppy is accustomed to dropping to blanks, the gun itself may be introduced. The first lesson must be devoted to putting the gun to the shoulder and swinging it as for shooting. If the puppy shows no sign of alarm at this innovation, well and good. In practice it will often do so, however, for this must naturally seem a most alarming procedure to it. The lesson must then simply be continued until the puppy is thoroughly accustomed to the sight of the gun being raised and swung. Blanks from the pistol may be fired at the same time to add realism, and the drop effected.

Only when the puppy is judged completely ready for it should the gun be fired and the puppy dropped to the sound of shot when quartering. From then onwards, however, the gun may be used increasingly frequently and shots fired occasionally to ensure that this important lesson is thoroughly learned. In this connection I am against the practice of teaching the puppy to drop to the raised gun as this is liable to distract the puppy's attention from its quartering. In any case with the above method of training it is redundant. The puppy soon learns to anticipate the shot, if it sees the gun being raised, without being taught.

The query most people seem to ask about this system of training is why two signals are used for teaching the puppy to sit. The answer is that later on there are occasions when the raised hand is preferable to the stamped foot and vice versa. This is simply my own personal view, but in practice I have found it sound. The choice of all commands and signals must be a purely personal one and so long as there is no confusion in the dog's mind it does not matter, within reason, what the trainer uses.

The most common resistance that people seem to come up against in the preliminary training is that of the puppy refusing to come when called. This is usually due to the puppy having been beaten or reprimanded unduly on coming to heel. This is, of course, fatal. Should the trainer have allowed himself to get into the false position whereby the puppy is free and refusing to obey the command 'Heel' or hand signal, it must on no account be shouted at or chased. If the situation is completely ignored and the trainer continues on his or her way repeating the command 'Heel' at intervals it is probable that the puppy will obey.

Should this not at once prove successful the trainer should try to get between the puppy and its kennel and return to the kennel first. If, however, the puppy gets to the kennel first the trainer must stand over it and place it in position while repeating the command 'Heel'. He would be then well advised to slip on the lead and give a short sharp walk repeating the command 'Heel' at intervals before returning the puppy to the kennel. There should then be subsequent lessons on a check lead before the puppy is allowed off again.

The main mistake here is punishing the puppy in such a way that it has come to associate punishment with coming to heel. If taught properly the puppy should always come to heel gladly and be acknowledged with a cheerful word of praise in the early stages, but the training should never be allowed to degenerate into a game. Nor should the puppy ever be allowed to realise that it has disobeyed and been successful in its disobedience. Should the puppy stray from heel without permission and refuse to return it is useless to raise your voice or lose your temper. The idea of conveying to the puppy that there is always an invisible bond of control between it and the trainer is all important. A word of encouragement accompanied by a quick change of direction will probably bring the puppy running. Another change of direction and the puppy's attention can be gained again. As soon as possible the check lead should then be slipped on and an opportunity for repetition of the disobedience given so that appropriate counter measures may be taken.

In these first lessons with a headstrong puppy it is often worth giving him a chance to run free disobediently with the check cord in position. A sharp tug and he will tumble head over heels. Even in the most obstinate cases it is unnecessary to do this more than once or twice. It does not hurt the puppy but it does give him a surprise and fosters the idea that the trainer is able to control him at a distance. It is this idea that should be implanted in the puppy's mind from the start.

In order to enhance this impression of always being in control it is best to ignore temporary lapses or mistakes on the puppy's part to begin with. Even attempted disobedience should sometimes be completely overlooked rather than give the puppy an order that cannot be enforced. As soon as control has been re-established, however, the lesson should be run through again and any repetition of the attempted disobedience promptly curbed.

The greatest difficulty most people seem to have in this stage of training is in keeping the puppy in to heel. Indoor practice in a room or corridor where the walls force the

puppy to maintain position is often a sound means of
driving the lesson home, but absolute insistence on position
can be overdone. Outside, in the early stages, all walking
with the puppy at heel must be done at a smart pace and
an aid to positioning such as a fence or wall is useful.
The puppy is then forced to maintain its station at heel
and is unable to slip past or wander. The faster the pace
the less chance there is of the puppy's attention being
distracted.

Of course the Pointer-Retriever is meant to range
freely and it is most important not to curb his natural
initiative. This is where a fine balance must be struck.
Some people advocate for this reason that the primary
obedience training should not be taught too young lest
the natural instinct be dulled. There is always a danger of
this with the heavy-handed trainer or the sensitive puppy,
but I cannot personally agree that training of this nature
should be left until later. It is imperative, however, that
due account be taken of the puppy's age and temperament
and that free ranging be encouraged alternately with the
lessons.

The tendency with the likely Pointer-Retriever puppy
is instinctively to range in front from the earliest days,
quartering the ground after a fashion at speed. This is
naturally to be encouraged. Should the puppy lag behind
it is to be urged on ahead with a wave of the hand and
the command 'Cast on'. Remember, however, that the
young dog should never be allowed to exhaust itself. A
quarter of an hour of full-speed ranging at a time is
ample unless the puppy is to be allowed to degenerate
into a pottering slowcoach.

It is as well that the trainer of the Pointer-Retriever
should consider the matter of distance during these early
lessons. If he paces out and marks fifty and hundred yard
intervals and notes the size and appearance of the puppy,

at a later date over those distances he will soon become accustomed to working out automatically how far away the puppy is ranging. It is imperative that the trainer should know how far away his puppy is at all times.

The distance the dog may range later on in practice must vary with the ground as I have already indicated. In thick cover ten yards either side of the handler or even less might suffice. In light open ground eighty to a hundred yards either side of the handler might be correct. It will be realised that this means that a line of five guns thirty yards apart is being more than amply covered by one dog. I feel personally that in no circumstances should the dog be ranging regularly more than forty yards in front of the handler and at no time should distances much greater than those mentioned either side of the handler be encouraged, unless in exceptional circumstances. For the average roughshooter and dog these ranges should be more than ample.

It must be appreciated that as the range varies so the pace should vary also. Clearly if the dog is ranging twenty yards to either side it should be moving slower than when it is ranging eighty yards to either side, unless it is covering a great deal of ground unnecessarily. Of course with an inexperienced young dog little in the way of variation in pace is likely, but it seems to me that no dog could be expected to cover a greater area of ground than has been suggested without moving at a speed which is likely to be too fast for its nose, causing it to miss game. If it does cover a larger area it is also likely to be outside effective controlling range. This is, however, a subject on which people have very different ideas and it must be left to the trainer to check his distances for himself and decide from his own handling and his own dog's capabilities what is correct.

At this stage of training the question is largely academic.

The puppy naturally cannot be expected to start polished ranging and quartering immediately and little attempt should be made to teach it at this stage. This primary obedience training may be considered successfully completed when the puppy is ranging freely, if wildly, and dropping at command, signal, shot or whistle, then continuing to range or returning promptly to heel at command, or signal, and walking to heel smartly; sitting automatically when the trainer halts; staying put to command, or signal, while the trainer walks out of sight, then coming promptly at command or whistle. This is the basis on which all subsequent training is founded. If this foundation is not securely laid, certain trouble is bound to ensue.

FOUR

First stages in Retrieving and Steadiness

FIRST SOME comments on retrieving. I imagine most roughshooters and gundog owners will agree with me that there are few sights more thrilling and satisfying than watching your own dog carry out a really difficult retrieve on a strong runner. Perhaps the only sight to equal it is to see a well trained general purpose Pointer-Retriever carrying out a perfect point and flush prior to the retrieve itself. Certainly the combination in one dog makes a most impressive spectacle and any difficulties experienced in training seem at once worthwhile.

The important things required from any dog in a retrieve are speed, certainty, steadiness and, above all, a soft mouth. There should be no slow uncertain snuffling progress which can be so frustrating to watch, but nor on the other hand should the dog be dashing round wildly in circles, head in the air, hoping to catch the scent or see his quarry moving. The dog should move obediently and eagerly in the direction indicated by his handler, make a quick find and a smooth pick up, followed by a speedy return and a clean delivery. While following the trail of wounded game comes at a later stage the puppy can be trained up to a very high degree of proficiency in retrieving without ever having in fact retrieved more than the dummy.

It is by using the puppy too early on real game, or by careless handling, or improper training that many puppies are spoiled. If a puppy of any breed is taken out too soon with the real thing, or if, conversely, it has over-much dummy practice, it is liable to become hard-mouthed: in the latter case from sheer boredom. Later on in the field a panicky dispatch after wounded game still in sight should never be allowed, nor should the dog be made to pick up game lying in full view in the open. Both these all too common practices lead to mouthing and inefficient retrieving, for, if the young dog can see the game, clearly it is liable to use its eyes rather than its nose and run in with over much enthusiasm and effect a slovenly pick up with danger of nipping the game.

Used solely as a retriever the Pointer-Retriever should be able to sit at heel and mark the game as it falls. He should then be able to retrieve birds as indicated from memory. Used in front in his Pointer-Retriever role his task is in many ways more difficult since there is more temptation in his way. Once he has pointed the game and flushed it to command he must go down automatically and wait for the order to retrieve to be given.

Here at once the great danger with the Pointer-Retriever is apparent. He must wait for the order to retrieve, however great the temptation to run in may be. Out in front as he is, the temptation is many times greater than for the dog at heel, but the cardinal rule must be that he remains down without running in. If the primary obedience training has not been properly carried out this is where the rest founders. For if the puppy will drop to command, signal and shot and stay put, it can soon be trained to drop to game flushed and game shot in the open as part of its training for steadiness in retrieving. This is in fact nothing more than an advanced form of obedience training carried one stage further, but the puppy must be reliable on the primary obedience training and retrieving training itself must come first.

In order to achieve this steadiness all dummy training must be carried out as nearly as possible to emulate the real thing. In practice, as will be explained, there is no great difficulty in reproducing conditions as near to those which may be expected as necessary. But remember that dead game should not be used with too young a dog in case bad habits are formed by accident. To begin with I always use a well filled sock dummy, which does no harm if the milk teeth catch in it; a man's stocking stuffed with sheepskin or something similar weighing about three pounds. It has the advantage that it is easily made to any size or weight, and it lasts better than almost anything else. A stuffed rabbit skin I do not like as it can cause mouthing when the dog is learning to flush game later or if torn accidentally. Of course, like any form of training, dummy retrieving must not be overdone. It is particularly important, once the day's lesson has been well learned, not to indulge in unnecessary dummy throwing and retrieving.

How then should retrieving practice start and when? The answer, as always, is that circumstances alter cases, but that generally speaking the instinct to retrieve is so deeply ingrained in most gundogs that they will start retrieving from the very beginning. There is a school of thought which holds that this should not be encouraged until the dog has been taught to point. My own feeling is that you should always encourage instinct, not try to stifle it or ignore it, or you will run into trouble.

The initial training is simplicity itself and if the puppy is kept in the house and insists on retrieving from an early age, there is no objection that I can see to making an especially small dummy for it and encouraging it along the right lines. A stuffed stocking weighing a couple of pounds will probably be about right to start with; heavy enough to prevent it being easily shaken and yet sufficiently light to be carried without strain.

The puppy is first given the command 'Sit' and the dummy is then thrown some four or five yards away in full view; the trainer standing with his back to the puppy's kennel or basket. Should the puppy try to run in after the dummy, as it probably will, it must be restrained with the commands 'No' and 'Sit' or a stamp of the foot, and, if necessary, a check lead to enforce them. After a few moments' restraint the command 'Hie Lost' is then given, accompanied by a wave of the hand to show what is intended.

Normally what happens is that the puppy goes to the dummy at once. As the puppy picks up the dummy, the trainer should recall it with the command and the hand signal, encouraging it verbally at the same time. As the puppy's instinct is to return with his prize to his kennel or basket, this will usually result in the puppy returning towards the trainer with the dummy, whereupon it should be intercepted and made much of as soon as it is within reach. On no account should the dummy be snatched or taken from the puppy at once, however. After a moment's interval the dummy may be gently removed. Should the puppy be unwilling to let it go a gentle pressure of the lips against the teeth will soon make him give it up. This should be accompanied by the word 'Dead'.

Should the puppy not go to the dummy at once or refuse to pick it up, the next step is to throw it and let the puppy go after it immediately. If the chasing instinct is encouraged by rolling an awkwardly shaped dummy, so that it bounces along the ground in a tantalising manner, so much the better. This will usually cause the puppy to run after it and pick it up, whereupon the puppy must be called and signalled to return, and encouraged verbally, as in the first instance. If all goes well, restraint may be applied the next time prior to the command 'Hie Lost', and so the puppy trained up by stages to waiting for the command to retrieve.

Some trainers believe in teaching the puppy to sit in front of his handler with the game held in his mouth until the handler accepts it. The idea behind this is to check over-impetuosity and I have found it extremely effective. It is always worth thinking, as has been indicated, in terms of what is being aimed at in training and dispensing with anything that is not strictly utilitarian. As a means of checking a high-spirited dog it is a sound practice to make him sit in front of you, or in the heel position as you prefer, before accepting the game. It is also helpful in checking any tendency to drop the game.

Initially, however, it may well be sufficient to train the puppy to retrieve to hand, holding the dummy until the command 'Dead'. Teaching it to 'Sit' while holding the dummy may come later. It is largely dependent on how much difficulty has been experienced so far. Personally I like to have the puppy sitting from the start if possible, but it must vary with the puppy and the circumstances as always.

It is important from the start to try to emulate work in the field as far as possible. A mistake many people make is to bend down and accept the game with both hands. While this may be permissible in the very early stages it should be discontinued as soon as possible. Only one hand can be used in the field without laying down the gun and should the puppy come to expect both, it may refuse to retrieve to one only. Nor is it wise to stand erect staring at the puppy as it approaches. The power of the human eye is often exaggerated but it must always be remembered that the puppy is extremely easily put off in the early stages and, especially to begin with, it is advisable to keep the head down and the eyes averted to encourage the puppy to come close to your hand with the dummy.

Failure to pick up the dummy, or dropping it some distance from the trainer, or circling the trainer are the most common resistances that are likely to be encountered. Complete failure to retrieve is not unknown, but it is unlikely in a dog with instinct inbred. It may be due to some incident in puppyhood such as the harsh removal of a slipper and a beating for chewing it. Hence the need for the careful handling of the potential gundog from the start. There are puppies, however, that refuse to retrieve without endless trouble on the part of the trainer and there are some that have to remain untaught.

The main secret of teaching retrieving in stubborn cases is to find something that the puppy is prepared to pick up in its mouth at once. A toy may be given to the puppy to play with for this express purpose, though care must be taken that this does not lead to mouthing and shaking. Once the puppy is keen to pick up some such object in its mouth half the battle is over.

I do not advocate the method of the forced retrieve which is used by some trainers. In this method a dummy is forcibly held in the puppy's mouth and physical pain is sharply applied to a part of the dog's anatomy (e.g. the ear pinched tightly) to make the jaws close. As soon as the dummy is held the pain is relieved and the puppy is made much of, but if the dummy is then dropped the process is repeated, ad infinitum. Like the use of a twitch on a horse it may work, but it frequently only makes matters worse and there are better ways of getting the same result without the puppy losing confidence in its trainer. Like most short cuts this probably proves more trouble in the long run.

In really difficult cases patience is the only answer, but sometimes a complete change of scene and method works surprisingly well. For instance the method of taking the young dog out in a boat on a lake and throwing the dummy from the boat might be tried. With a keen water dog this might work. Though this is not a method I would normally recommend, it is one way of teaching retrieving and it has the advantage that the dog must swim back to the boat. In this as in all methods of training a careful study of the individual dog must be made.

Should the puppy start to drop the dummy in front of you the worst thing you can do is advance and pick it up. Instead take a couple of paces sharply backwards and repeat the command 'Hie Lost' if necessary, or otherwise encourage the puppy verbally, keeping the head averted all the time. In practice the puppy will usually pick up the dummy again and this time hold it until the command 'Dead' is given. Should the puppy again drop it, another couple of paces backwards and more verbal encouragement should cause the puppy to pick it up once more. If, however, the puppy still shows signs of dropping it, a half turn and a show of walking away are usually enough to cause it to hold on to the dummy. It is probably the best plan then, however, to walk away encouraging the puppy to follow with the dummy in its mouth until it realises that the dummy must be held until the command 'Dead'.

An advance towards the puppy when it is hesitating about retrieving or when it has dropped the dummy is almost always a fatal move. The puppy may think it is a game and snatch at the dummy and run away with it, thus developing a resistance to delivering to hand, or if the dummy is removed it may develop a resistance to re-trieving. It sometimes happens in this connection that the puppy on exercise gets hold of some old decayed relic or even sometimes a crippled bird or animal. In the early stages, at any rate, this should be treated as a dummy and the puppy should be encouraged to deliver it to hand rather than risk causing a resistance to retrieving. (Later on, of course, a firm warning 'No' should be sufficient). In almost every instance where hesitation is shown about returning with the dummy it is better to walk away from the puppy than towards it if verbal encouragement shows no sign of being immediately successful.

Another tiresome habit that the puppy will sometimes develop is that of circling the trainer with the dummy in its mouth. This can be caused by staring at a sensitive youngster as it approaches, but circumventing it is easy enough. By standing with the back to a wall, or in a confined space, such as a wired run, or corridor, the trainer can leave the puppy no alternative but to come to him direct.

It must be emphasised that while these faults may be cured in puppies they are all too common in adult retrievers of any breed and are usually due to the same cause. If the dog is beaten for running in to retrieve on its return with the game, then it will naturally connect that beating with the retrieving and not with the running in. The handler must always be alive to the effect of his actions on the dog. Punishment must always be directly connected with offence without any possibility of doubt to the dog's mind. A puppy may be trained comparatively simply, but it is a different matter trying to re-train an adult dog, or a spoiled puppy. The old trite saying "Months to make and moments to spoil" is unfortunately only too true.

In practice, normally, little difficulty should be experienced in getting the puppy to fetch the dummy at the word of command. To begin with, however, the trainer should be satisfied if the retrieve is made straight to him without shaking or mouthing. He should also be satisfied if the puppy delivers freely to hand. In due course he will be able to get the puppy to sit before he accepts the

dummy and add the other refinements which are to be
desired. It is always to be remembered that the puppy
can be easily confused and when it does the job correctly
it should be made much of and not pressed to repeat the
performance unnecessarily.

Nor must the early retrieves be made too difficult. To
start with, the puppy should always see the dummy
thrown and be able to mark the fall. Only in the very
earliest stages of all, however, and in the case of a well
grown puppy full of instinct, possibly not even then,
should the dummy be thrown so that it remains in full
view. Otherwise, as has been pointed out, there is danger
of the puppy running in over enthusiastically and
learning slipshod habits. The dummy should be thrown
so that it lands in stubble or grass and is concealed from
view. The trainer may then encourage the puppy to
retrieve with outstretched arm as well as command.

In a surprisingly short time the trainer will be able to
indicate a direction with outstretched arm and the
command 'Hie Lost' and the puppy will go off and
return with the dummy. In this game of 'Hunt the
dummy' the puppy will be keen to join. Each day the
commands so far learned should be used in a general
revision, making a mock field day out of each day's
exercise. On walking to heel the foot is stamped and the
puppy sits automatically. Then with a wave of the hand
and the command 'Hie Lost' he is sent after a dummy
previously concealed up-wind. In this way the training
advances, but always at the pace of the puppy.

At this stage an assistant can be made useful by throwing
the dummy from concealed positions at a given signal
from the trainer. Also a gun should normally be carried
from this stage onwards to accustom the puppy to field
conditions. It will be recalled that the puppy has already
been accustomed to the noise and movement of the gun,

while being taught to drop to shot during its primary obedience training. Therefore, when the appearance of the dummy in the air in front of it is greeted with a shot, the puppy should automatically drop. If he does not do so immediately the command 'Sit' must be rapped out in time to prevent him running in, or recourse will have to be made to the check cord again. After a suitable interval the command 'Hie Lost' may be given.

The next stage or extension of this part of the training requires several specially made dummies which are not meant to be retrieved. There are several ways of making these but the prime essential is that they should roll in an irregular manner with a series of tantalising hops and jumps in the manner of a hare starting from its form or a rabbit twisting and turning amid tufts of grass. I used to use an old croquet ball with two or three football boot studs and a few old rabbit tails nailed to it, but there is no need for anything so elaborate. A suitable knobbly shaped turnip, or a sawn log of wood about six inches in diameter by two or three inches across is quite sufficient. The whole essence of them is to attract the dog to run in by emulating the tantalising hops and twists of a fleeing rabbit or hare. It is surprising how effective they are.

The puppy should be accustomed to these dummies by having one or two rolled past its nose from a concealed position while it is on the check lead. Should it evince any desire to run after them it must be sternly checked. The next time the dummy may be greeted with a shot and the puppy made to drop. Only when the puppy appears completely steady and drops at the sight of the dummies should they be tried out in the open.

The best place for this type of training is a piece of park land with a number of trees dotted about at suitable intervals behind which the assistant can stand concealed preparatory to bowling these dummies past the puppy's

nose. It is to be remembered that the puppy will soon
scent the assistant if he stands up wind so that the advance
must be made down wind towards the assistant. As soon
as the dummy appears, the trainer may greet it with a shot
and soon the puppy will be dropping as much to the
appearance of the dummy, or anything moving in front of
him, as to the shot or command.

This is probably the most important lesson in steadiness
the puppy has to learn. Apart from learning to drop to
flushed game the puppy also learns that it has to await the
trainer's wishes as to what it shall retrieve. Remember,
however, that with this training as with any other the
puppy's interest must be maintained. It is not reasonable
to expect too much or too speedy an advance. Once the
puppy has performed this lesson perfectly do not go on
repeating it until the puppy breaks after the dummy from
sheer boredom to relieve the monotony. Give it a chance
then to retrieve the other dummy and add interest and
variety to its training. Once performed well is probably
quite sufficient for the first time.

It need scarcely be pointed out that although this
lesson is really only a form of advanced primary obedience
training it is important to leave it until the puppy has
learned to retrieve reliably. Obviously otherwise there is
a danger of confusing the puppy unnecessarily and
possibly setting up a resistance to retrieving.

Although this is one of the most vital lessons of this
stage there are still some important points about retrieving to be learned. Firstly the puppy must be sent to
retrieve a dummy in the normal fashion, then as it returns
another dummy must be thrown to one side so that the
puppy is tempted to drop the one in its mouth and pick
up the other. How often otherwise perfect retrieves have
been spoiled by the dog hesitating as another bird fell and
sometimes making the mistake of dropping the bird it

carried, then finally retrieving neither! Any attempt to do so must of course be nipped in the bud with a stern 'No'. Similarly if the puppy shows any inclination to go down it must be encouraged to return to heel. Should the dummy be dropped, the puppy must be encouraged to retrieve it to hand and the lesson repeated until it is thoroughly learned. The puppy will soon realise that when retrieving nothing must deflect it from its purpose.

The next stage of this lesson is throwing yet another third dummy on the other side of the puppy as it retrieves the first. By this time there should be no hesitation on the puppy's part. On retrieving the first dummy it may be sent back with the trainer's outstretched arm pointing in the direction of the second dummy. Should it show any hesitation about which dummy to fetch the trainer's meaning must be made clear to it by a warning 'No' if it approaches the wrong one. In this way it soon learns to follow the direction of the trainer's outstretched arm.

In conjunction with this training a dummy may be thrown to one side when walking with the warning 'No' to the puppy and then 'Mark'. The walk may then be continued for a little way and the command 'Hie Lost' given. In a surprisingly short while two or more dummies can be thrown and marked. Each in turn may be indicated with the trainer's arm held out and retrieved. In this way the puppy learns to memorise and distinguish different dummies as later he will have to memorise and distinguish different birds.

As the puppy's standard advances, so the ground chosen for these exercises may become more difficult. Starting with the very first lesson in the open where the dummies may be easily found and retrieved, the puppy may be introduced speedily to long grass and stubble, then gradually to thicker cover. Similarly instead of the wind making it easy for him to find the dummies they may be thrown to windward so that he has to hunt for them. All the time the difficulty of the tasks set should be steadily increasing, but never so that there is any danger of the puppy becoming discouraged.

Apart from cover hazards, now is the time to introduce the puppy to water hazards. It is important to start him off mildly. Nothing is more calculated to put any puppy off than being hurled unexpectedly into icy water or thrown into the middle of a gorse bush. No one in their senses would expect these methods to do anything but cause the puppy to have an aversion to water and cover thereafter. Yet that is the way some people would set about it.

By the common-sense approach of starting off in shallow water and working up to deeper pools and fast-running rivers the puppy can be encouraged to make retrieves both in and across the water. In the same way the density of the cover may be neatly worked up from bracken and long grass to brambles and gorse, all the time with the incentive of the dummy to fetch.

So far it must be clear that all the training has been leading up to the real thing. The training has been gradual but the progress has been continuous. The puppy should now be carrying out difficult retrieves amidst cover or across water in the desired manner, sitting in front of the trainer and making a clean delivery. His memory training should have been begun and he should be able to watch several dummies being thrown and mark them, retrieving each at indication. Above all he should now be steady in front of the gun, dropping at the sight of anything moving, or the dummy being 'flushed'.

At the same time the other aspects of the puppy's training have not been neglected. Primary obedience has been checked regularly in daily exercise and the use of hand signals should have improved the quartering of the ground. The puppy's education has now reached the stage of pointing.

There is one school of thought which says firmly that all this training so far should have been held up until the Pointer-Retriever has been taught to point. Then and then only, they say, should the serious training start. The two things are separate and distinct and, they maintain, must be kept apart so that there is no confusion in the Pointer-Retriever's mind. This, however, seems to me to be faulty reasoning.

I quite agree that the two aspects of training must be kept separate. There must clearly never be any confusion in the puppy's mind between its duties in quartering the ground, game finding and pointing, and its duties in retrieving game when shot. But training properly executed by the means I have indicated should cause no confusion in the puppy's mind. So far the puppy has merely had every lesson in steadiness instilled without seeing a shot fired in earnest. Nor will I admit that a spirited puppy has had its initiative in any way cramped by not being permitted to range freely at all times. It has merely been well trained in basic steadiness and had its natural retrieving ability encouraged.

While I do not agree that pointing must come first I do agree that, to begin with, it must be kept separate, for there is one big difference between the training that is to come and the training that has taken place already. All the training so far has been on dummies. The time has come at last for the first approach to the real thing. When it comes to teaching game finding and pointing the only way for the puppy to learn is on live game.

FIVE

On Scent and Scenting, Gamefinding, Pointing and Flushing

THE PUPPY has now begun to approach that stage of steadiness which is to be expected from it later on. It is completely reliable on the basic obedience training. It drops at once to command, signal, whistle, shot and the dummy rolled in the manner of game flushed. It is a sound retriever, even though it has so far retrieved nothing other than the stuffed dummy. It is beginning to work well to hand signals. Yet, although all this has been achieved and a sound basic training has been absorbed, the scents of game have so far had no material part in the puppy's education. This is, therefore, the first step towards the real thing, for pointing cannot be taught, or the gamefinding instinct brought out, other than on live game.

It must be made clear at once, in case anyone is in any doubt on the subject, why live game is necessary. The scent of live game is different from that of dead or wounded game. It is important, to begin with, not to confu.e the puppy about scents and therefore only live game should be used at this stage. It is obviously not desirable to train the dog to point dead game, even if it can be done, and admittedly some puppies will point dead game at first. Later on dead game may be used to lay trails to teach the puppy to use its nose in advanced

retrieving prior to its real work in the field. But this is a
subject for the next chapter, when the puppy is already
steady on point and has begun to distinguish between the
meanings of the various scents more readily.

As yet the puppy will probably not have learned to
distinguish between the meanings of the various scents of
game at all, although this will come naturally to a large
extent with experience. However, quite apart from the
scents of the different types of game, the puppy must
learn to discriminate between air scent and foot scent.
Theoretically, of course, pointing will be done with the
head held high to catch the body scent of the game
carried by the air, and retrieving will be done with the
head down to follow the trail, or foot scent, left by the
feet of the game. But scent and scenting are matters
which seldom, if ever, allow themselves to be fitted into
rigid categories.

It must be obvious that clear-cut distinctions between
air scent and foot scent cannot always be expected. On
occasions the Pointer-Retriever may well be seen to
point with the head held low, or almost on top of the
game. At other times it will be obvious that a retrieve has
been made with the head held high following an air scent.

Nor must it be forgotten that, just as scent may vary,
so may the dog's powers of scenting as well (e.g. if the dog
is off colour). Admittedly the individual dog's scenting
powers may generally be accepted as fairly constant,
although variation between dogs may be considerable.
But it must be obvious that there are always a number of
variable outside factors affecting scent and scenting
which must also be brought into account. For clearly
as scent varies so the dog's scenting powers must be taxed
or favoured. It will be appreciated, therefore, that the
subject of scent and scenting often poses highly complex
problems, both to handler and dog.

It is most important that anyone who wishes to train or use a general purpose Pointer-Retriever should learn as much about the subject of scent and scenting as possible for themselves. I am personally convinced of only one thing, after studying the matter at length and watching different dogs' behaviour on many similar and sometimes apparently identical occasions, both in the matter of pointing and retrieving. I am convinced that no one can ever learn enough about this question. Too often the answers have to be guessed rather than proved and the only way to learn is by experience and observation. Experience in this context, and almost any other, I would define as the realisation of how little you know and an ever-readiness to learn more.

The ground, the wind and the weather, quite apart from the game and the dogs themselves, are the ever-variable factors affecting scent and scenting. In this country, though not always necessarily abroad, the ground, the wind and the weather are probably the most variable. As a matter of principle these are the factors which must be examined first on a shooting day. For on them to large extent must depend the scent and behaviour of the game and the scenting power of the dogs.

The ground itself may vary greatly in soil, growth or formation and it is impossible to separate it from the other two controlling factors of wind and weather. What may hold scent one day may not on the next and there may even be changes from hour to hour. It is impossible to lay down any hard and fast rules. The only true generalisation here is that extremes of wind or weather, whatever the ground, are not usually good for scent or scenting.

As regards both pointing and retrieving the important thing to remember is that game gives off different scents according to its condition and that these different scents themselves must vary with the ground, wind and weather conditions. Seldom, if ever, will game provide identical scent or scenting conditions. Sometimes it will run ahead and at other times sit absolutely tight without movement. Sometimes foot scent may be carried by the air and at other times body scent may hardly be carried at all. Then again sick or wounded game may have an entirely different scent both from each other and from healthy game.

Any game that is frightened will usually give off a very distinctive fear scent and usually when game is flushed it will defecate at once thus ridding itself of an unnecessary encumbrance in its flight. It is probable incidentally that these two factors are related and have some bearing on the occasional wounded bird which mysteriously disappears leaving apparently no scent at all. Over a number of years shooting I have never noted such a bird which had not been shot from behind thus indicating that the fear scent had in some way been blocked.

In any case since both the scent and scenting of game are necessarily governed by the terrain and vegetation which may be good for holding scent or again may not, and since these in turn are governed by the wind and the weather, it will be appreciated that there are an infinite variety of considerations to be taken into account. It will be obvious, too, that all the factors affecting scent and scenting are inextricably inter-related and it is impossible to do more than generalise on the subject. Scent and scenting must be dependent on the game, the ground, the time of day and year, the wind and the weather, but most of all on the dog. A dog with a good nose and good scenting capabilities will make the most of a poor scent and bad conditions, whereas the dog with a poor nose and indifferent scenting capabilities will not be greatly helped by good conditions.

It is very difficult for us with our miserable limitations in this faculty of scenting to understand what it must be like for the puppy. There must be so many new and tempting scents which all cry out for investigation. Then, as the puppy gradually begins to learn their meanings, is the time to start instilling the lesson that pointing is required. Deeply hidden though the instinct may be, it is usually possible to bring it to the fore. Once again it is impossible to lay down any hard and fast rules, but if the breed of dog is such that pointing might be expected to be a highly developed instinct it might be advisable to wait to see whether it begins to manifest itself. As with retrieving, however, there can be no certain method which ensures success, even in a dog of a breed recognised as possessing the instinct to a marked degree.

The point itself is literally an arresting spectacle. The handler's attention is attracted willy-nilly by the rigid pose. Whether the forefoot is held up for feather and the hind for fur, as is frequently the case, scarcely matters. Sometimes all four feet will be firmly on the ground and the head crooked at an odd angle backwards when game has been almost overshot. At other times the classical pose of body, head and tail in a straight line will be seen. Do not, however, listen to those who enthuse about the grace and beauty of the point. Very often it is far from beautiful, but, whatever it may look like, it is always arresting.

From a utilitarian angle it is worth while attempting to school your puppy to raise certain feet for certain types of game, i.e. fore for feather, hind for fur. But it is too much to expect him to do it every time. All that can be done is to train him by raising the required paw by hand when he is on point to the appropriate artificially introduced substitute for wild game. This can be done surprisingly easily. In practice thereafter it is usually a case of accepting and applauding the perfect point when it comes and being grateful for sound work in finding the game otherwise. It is useless to expect aesthetic perfection every time.

For training purposes I do not think it matters which is used first, whether feather or fur. I know this may cause an outcry amongst some purists, but my answer is simple. These dogs are going to be used in front, anyway, and of necessity they must learn steadiness on fur as well as feather from the start. I would point out, however, that I do not advocate that any game should be shot over them at this stage. As has been emphasised before, the whole basis of this method of training is founded on keeping the dog in ignorance of the killing power of the gun until, to all intents and purposes, he is already fully trained.

The object of the first stage of this training is to teach the puppy to find the game and to come rigidly on point on scenting it and to remain rigidly on point until ordered to flush it. The second stage of the training is to teach the puppy to flush the game without any attempt at mouthing. In both stages the puppy must go down when the game is flushed and must then wait steadily for the order to retrieve. (It will of course be appreciated that the groundwork for this last lesson has already been well laid).

The ground for practice does not need to be elaborate. Wired-in enclosures and tame rabbits are not by any means essential and in many ways better dispensed with entirely. The nearer every aspect of training can be kept to the real thing the better. I used to have a small and rabbity wood nearby where certain tufts of cover could be guaranteed to hold a rabbit at certain periods of the day. Now I usually work on game in the open. It is easy enough on most shoots to mark places where game is in the habit of lying and to walk the dog up on them.

In any case of difficulty with a puppy, or where game is scarce and wild and there is little time to spare, it is

arly dummy retrieve.

itial retrieving—ignoring temptation; one dummy on right and
e on left—back to wall and eyes averted.

Learning to drop to rolled dummy: assistant should be well concealed.

usually helpful, however, to place artificially introduced substitutes for wild game on the ground. There are several methods of doing this. Most game birds can be rendered temporarily unconscious by rocking quickly for a minute or two with the head tucked under the wing and then placing them gently on their backs. The effect is much the same as hypnotising a cockerel by placing it nose down on a white line. Pigeons especially can be laid on their backs for periods of up to a quarter of an hour or more without stirring. They will probably need a sharp prod to disturb them and for this reason they are perfect for teaching the puppy gamefinding and pointing in the first stage and to flush game in the second stage.

The only problem with this method is finding the game to use, since once it is flushed it should be allowed to fly off freely. The old poacher's trick of feeding grain soaked in alcohol is one way of providing a supply, but the best and simplest answer is to find someone who keeps pigeons. A dovecot in the garden is even better. The birds can then be easily caught, as and when required, and, once having served their purpose and been flushed, they return home under their own power, none the worse, to be used again another day.

Another method of artificially introducing a substitute for wild game is the use of game in cages. This is rather akin to the old method of training a retriever in steadiness by walking up a line of knotted rabbit snares. Although gamefinding and steadiness on point can be taught this way I do not favour it, as I think the cages are liable to interfere with the scent so that it is less reliable than dizzied pigeons or game. Also, of course, and more important still, the game cannot be flushed.

Yet another method is to use tethered game. If birds are to be used they should be pinioned as well, with a rubber band round the body, or they will tend to flutter their wings. With tame rabbits or hares a harness may be devised and according to the length of tether the game can be flushed. I must make it clear, however, that I do not approve of this method either, since, even more than caged game, it always savours of cruelty to me. Nor is it either efficient or reliable since the game is very likely to attract attention to itself by making efforts to escape. The dizzied pigeon is by far the best artificial method, both from a humane and practical viewpoint.

It is desirable, however, in all matters of training, to approach as near to reality as possible. For this reason I advocate working on wild game in the open whenever feasible. The use of an old dog may be an advantage then, to find the exact position of the game, so that the approach can be made with the puppy under absolute control, but it is by no means a necessity. In the early part of the year paired birds, for instance, will usually sit very tight and provide a ready means of training the youngster.

The method of introducing the puppy to game, whether it is wild game, or the artificially introduced substitute, must vary with the degree of control that the trainer feels he has attained and the degree of instinct that the puppy is showing. If the puppy is thoroughly steady and reliable on its primary obedience training and the pointing instinct is obviously highly developed, then it may be allowed to quarter freely on wild game; the game being upwind. If on the other hand the trainer is doubtful and wishes to be absolutely sure of bringing his puppy on steadily under control, then artificially introduced substitutes and the check lead may be advisable. The former method is certainly preferable, if possible, as the more freedom the puppy may be allowed in training the better.

Whichever method is used, it must be appreciated that one of two things may happen. The puppy will either point instinctively and rigidly when it scents the game or it will rush blindly into it and flush it. In the first instance, which it is to be hoped will arise, all is easy. In the second instance the puppy should go down automatically on seeing the game flushed in front of it. Should it not do so an instant command must be rapped out. The puppy must never be allowed to run in persistently after flushed game. If it does so, resort to the check cord must be made once again.

Taking it that on scenting the game the puppy has frozen into an instant point, the rest is simple enough. The important thing to remember now is that the puppy is working instinctively. It does not even as yet know why it is pointing. Instinct has told it to go rigid and it has simply obeyed. It is quite probable that spoken orders will have no effect on the puppy at this stage, so deeply has instinct gripped it. This is in fact all to the good as it means it will almost certainly develop into a steady and reliable pointer.

Care must be taken at this stage to stand absolutely still at first. Should the puppy show any tendency to move forward the word 'No' must be repeated softly in warning tones. Only when the puppy is standing staunchly should the trainer advance slowly and cautiously. By this time the puppy will be firmly rigid and as the check lead is slipped on it should be gently stroked to show appreciation of its work. Nothing can be more calculated to upset the point than the immediate and precipitate advance of the trainer to check his puppy. The effect is usually diametrically opposed to that intended.

It may be that the puppy is still not absolutely rigid but advances slowly like a moving statue. The command 'No' should then be given, as has been indicated, to check any sign of impulsiveness. If necessary, pressure on the check lead must be used to show that the movement is not desired. After a suitable pause the command 'Set Up' may

be given in firm tones, accompanied by a forward movement of the hand from the hip to shoulder level. This
should have the double effect of flushing the game and
causing the puppy to go down. The natural confusion in
the puppy's mind between 'Set' and 'Sit' is likely to make
the puppy go down more readily, even if the flushed
game does not cause him to do so. Very soon the dual
command can be dispensed with and the single command
'Up' may be used for flushing, accompanied always by
the hand signal.

This performance must be repeated several times, it
being borne in mind that the puppy should always be
encouraged to road out (work out) the scent after dropping
to flush, to ensure that the game has all gone. Generally
the lesson will be absorbed by an apt pupil surprisingly
quickly, but it is possible that the puppy may be over-
impulsive. If this is the case the check lead may be re-
introduced and the puppy held in position as suggested
with the command 'No' until it is rigid on point.

The other possibility which is likely to arise is that of
the puppy which does not come on point at all and shows
no sign of doing so. Should it merely flush the game it will,
however, almost certainly halt and must then be made to
drop. The best principle is to repeat this performance also
a number of times. If the instinct is there it is very likely
to be encouraged by this means. Should the puppy still
show no sign of pointing, the wisest course may be to
wait until it is older to see whether the instinct manifests
itself later.

If, however, the trainer decides to go ahead with the
training, it is advisable to use artificially introduced
substitutes for wild game and advance with the puppy on
the check lead as indicated. Then, as soon as the trainer
judges that the scent of the game must have reached the
puppy, he must give the command 'Steady' and advance

slowly with the puppy held firmly. If allowed to do so the puppy would often almost bump noses with the game, but the trainer must check it finally some way short of this stage and hold it rigidly on the lead with a warning 'No'. It should then be gently stroked from head to tail to show that this is what is required.

The training then continues, if possible, as before with the command 'Up' being given, the game being flushed and the puppy going down, then in due course being encouraged to road out the scent. If this is not possible, due to the use of caged game, then this part of the training must be held over until the puppy points reliably. With careful repetition even the dog to which pointing is not instinctive may be taught in this manner to point, if not rigidly, at least standing staunchly with tail just moving. But this is not to say that there are not occasions when this will fail. No methods are infallible and there are bound to be exceptions to every rule. It is merely suggested that this is a sound method of training and is likely to be successful even in cases that at first appear doubtful. Of course where the puppy really has no natural ability or where it has already been spoiled through earlier bad handling, nothing much can be expected. The answer is not to try to train dogs which show no natural inclination or which have been spoiled by someone else's bad handling. Any trainer will agree with these sentiments.

The most likely resistances are first and foremost a tendency to rush in on the game and attempt to seize it. This may be due to having been allowed to retrieve wounded game at some time, or possibly to some accidental happening when the puppy has been able to mouth live game. The only way to overcome this tendency is to continue on practice with the check lead and artificially introduced substitutes for wild game until the puppy thoroughly appreciates what is required. This may require much patience and a good supply of pigeons, but in practice it is surprising how efficient this method can be.

A similar resistance, which is more readily cured, is a persistent tendency to draw on. The dog will come on point but, either at once or by degrees, advances until the game is flushed. This is probably due to the handler having advanced too quickly towards the point and it can become a tiresome and annoying habit. The cure is again the check lead and artificially introduced substitutes for wild game.

More difficult to cure are the habits a dog may develop of lying down when coming on point, or of breaking off the point and returning to the handler (known as blinking). These may be due to harsh treatment, to gun-shyness, or to training with an older dog, or to over-training, probably on artificially introduced substitutes for wild game, with resultant confusion in the dog's mind. Just as some people cannot resist throwing the dummy to see their dog retrieve, so others will persist in bringing their dog on point on artificially introduced substitutes for wild game. It cannot be over-emphasised that no training lesson should ever be laboured until there is danger of the dog being sickened. It must also be realised that when-ever the dog comes on point it is desirable that the handler should approach and see the game flushed correctly. Ignoring a dog's points, or persistently calling a dog off point, can sour a dog as effectively as overtraining and cause blinking.

The best answer in such cases is to give the dog a complete rest from pointing and indeed from work of any kind for a while. If the dog is first encouraged to work as a retriever in the field and is then brought back to pointing, on wild game if possible or in as realistic conditions as can be achieved if not, a cure may be effected. Any tendency to drop must be checked at once. If necessary the handler must use the check cord to be right up with the dog as it comes on point. It may even be wise not to encourage the dog to drop on flushing game until this resistance has been overcome. The main difficulty here is probably to regain the dog's enthusiasm for its work.

False pointing, or pointing where no game lies, is also a common failing in the youngster, although not strictly speaking a resistance. Usually it is merely a question of the young dog not having learned fully to discriminate between scents. It will freeze on point at a scent which an older dog would recognise as being too faint to be worth noting. Especially towards the end of the shooting season, when the birds are wild and do not remain in one place for long, false pointing should be expected from the youngster and is nothing to worry about. Similarly pointing at larks is more than likely. There is something about a lark which will deceive most dogs, although it will usually be possible to tell from outward appearance whether the point is a genuine one or not.

As the handler becomes more accustomed to the dog's points and as the dog begins to learn scent discrimination, more and more can be learned from watching the point itself. A false point at a lark will probably be acknowledged with a faint wagging of the tail. A rabbit possibly in a similar way. A pheasant with a firm and rigid pose and partridge with head held high at a distance. Each point should indicate to the experienced eye what is in front. This individual understanding must of course vary with each dog and handler. A retriever which never quite reaches a fully rigid pose may well move its tail fast for rabbits and slowly for pheasants, or the reverse. Each dog will have its own methods of reacting which should soon be clear to the handler.

If either false pointing, or the opposite fault of missing game and failing to point (N.B. Also known sometimes as blinking), show signs of becoming a serious problem, even though the dog is given time to settle down, it may always, of course, be due to poor scenting capabilities. Tests on artificially introduced substitutes for wild game should soon decide the question. If there is nothing apparently wrong, except lack of scent discrimination, it should be well worth persevering with the dog. Possibly working him with an older dog will help matters. On the other hand if the dog's 'nose' is faulty there is no point in wasting further time with him.

The next stage is teaching the youngster to flush the game to command. There is the school of thought which maintains that the handler should always flush the game for the dog to maintain steadiness and reliability on point. Certainly with an excitable dog this may be sound in the early stages, but later on in the field the roughshooter is frequently not in a position to do the work for his dog, (e.g. in boggy ground, across ditches, etc.) and it is desirable that the dog should learn to flush the game to command. As in any case it will be expected to flush the game from cover and drop at once there is little more to teaching flushing in the open to command. But the dog must be steady on point first.

In practice in the normal course of events it should not be long before the puppy is quite steady on point. Then, and only then, to my mind should it be taught to move in to flush the game itself; it being emphasised here that so far all the game has been flushed, if it has been flushed, by the sound of the trainer's voice. Hence one of the advantages of using wild game. For this next stage, however, the artificially introduced pigeon is best employed.

In order to make sure that the puppy comes on point close enough to the bird it is advisable to quarter up-wind of it. In this way the puppy is likely to come on rigid point almost immediately on top of the bird rather than some yards from it. The puppy must then, after a suitable interval, be urged forward with the command 'Up' and the hand signal for flushing. On no account must mouthing be allowed. Should the puppy attempt to pick up the bird in its mouth a firm 'No' should be enough to show that this course of action is not desired.

If the puppy only does this once no harm should be suffered by either bird or puppy. If the puppy shows a tendency to persist in mouthing, however, a piece of string may be slipped loosely round the jaws while on point to act as a temporary muzzle, and resort made to the check lead again. The command 'Up' may then be given and the lesson will soon be understood. If a piece of string is used in this way it should be removed at once after the puppy has gone down. However it will probably not be necessary more than once.

It should not be long in practice before the puppy is thoroughly entering into the spirit of things to the extent of putting its nose beneath the game and giving it a powerful upward thrust. In some cases the puppy may take to bounding forward with the paws ahead to prod the game. This should be avoided, if possible, but there is probably no real harm in it so long as no attempt is made at mouthing or seizing the game.

In practice nine times out of ten the game will be flushed before the dog has had time to get within actual reach of it. The mere approach of the dog will suffice, for very often there is a form of hypnotic union established between the dog on point and the game and they will both remain rigid staring at each other until the dog moves to order and breaks the spell. Then the game will usually be off before the dog is within reach and the dog must, of course, drop. Should it be within the dog's power to seize the game it must understand that it is not to do so.

Here again it must be emphasised how important it is
that the puppy should not so far have retrieved wounded
game or learned the killing power of the gun. Meanwhile, but as an entirely separate part of its training, the
puppy can be carrying on its practice on dummy retrieving and all it has learned in primary obedience and
its other training so far.

It has already been stressed frequently that if at any
time the puppy shows signs of being bored or losing
interest, the training for the day should be promptly
packed up. However training with live game brightens
things up in a way that dummy training never can. It is
understandable why the puppy having reached this stage
of training should grow easily bored with the dummy and
begin to shake and worry it with very little warning.
Careful watch must be kept for fear of overdoing that
aspect of the training and causing this.

Here is where the amateur and the professional differ.
The professional has only so much time for each dog.
The amateur probably has all the time he wants. The
result is that the amateur with only one or two dogs may
easily overdo the training in his enthusiasm. The professional, if only by reason of the limited time he can spare
to each dog, is unlikely to do so. Furthermore the
professional probably knows more accurately and can
assess more readily when the dog has had enough, which
may not always be the case with the keen amateur.

The golden rule which has been stressed in these
chapters all the time is that training must never be
carried to excess. Once the lesson has been performed
adequately leave it at that for the moment. Even if it has
not been performed well or if some aspect of training
seems to be going thoroughly wrong (i.e. the dummy
being mouthed and shaken), it is often better to drop
training for the moment, sometimes for a period of

several days, and start completely afresh, rather than to go on and make matters worse.

To return to the pointing training, the puppy is now capable of being ranged freely ahead, finding the game and pointing, then flushing to order, and dropping, on live game, or on the artificially introduced substitutes. At this stage, while practising pointing, the puppy's quartering of the ground may be perfected. The puppy should now fully understand the meaning of the hand signals, extended full out for direction and down to the knee or thigh to come in closer or to heel, and its quartering is probably beginning to be reasonable.

The most likely faults are a tendency to turn back, instead of forward into the wind at each turn and quartering behind the guns. These, like ranging too far ahead, may be checked by hand signals easily enough. Lack of keenness, or over-training, or ranging too soon for too long periods may have caused the dog to show a tendency to remain too close to the trainer. This is best cured by two assistants walking one on either side of the trainer, the puppy being sent to each in turn while its range is gradually expanded. The opposite fault of ranging too far should be easily restricted to suitable limits by signal and whistle.

The trainer should now be in a position to judge the young dog's capabilities and to regulate its ranging in accordance with them. I will go into this subject at greater length in the chapter on use of the dogs, but at the moment I will merely repeat that I regard the maximum range the dog should be working in front as from forty to fifty yards and on either side as from eighty to a hundred. These distan :es must be regulated by the ground and the dog's ability and in most cases, in practice, they will almost certainly be a good deal less. It is obvious that the dog should not be ranged out of sight, otherwise his pointing ability is negatived and if greater distances than these have to be ranged to find game, then the ground needs re-stocking and somewhere else should be found to shoot in the meantime.

An important point here is that so far no effort has been made to train the puppy to cross fences, gates or hedges. The quartering can thus easily be regulated by ranging the puppy in suitably shaped fields. If none are available for any reason, resort may be had to suitably placed artificially introduced game. The puppy can then be placed by hand signals in the correct position to make a point. He thus learns early to pay attention to the whistle and to hand signals.

It might here be emphasised for those who criticise this training as reminiscent of semaphore and impracticable that I have never used anything else in practice either alone or in company. It is perfectly feasible with the gun held under one arm to signal with the other arm outstretched, and as the puppy's training improves the need to signal at all becomes less and less. At the same time the puppy begins of its own accord to regulate its pace in accordance with its ranging, as a variable-range, variable-pace Pointer-Retriever should.

In connection with the regulation of pace it is worth remembering that all walking at heel until this stage should have been carried out as fast as possible. Now the pace may be slowed down and varied, with the accompanying command 'Steady' if the puppy shows any inclination to move ahead out of station. But while it is important that the puppy should learn to vary its pace care must be taken not to overdo this training. Age and experience will be the puppy's best guides. It is better that the puppy should cover more ground than is strictly necessary than that it should cover too little with the danger of missing game. In due course as it learns what is required the young dog will automatically regulate its pace in accordance with its scenting ability and, as has been pointed out, this must vary with the scenting conditions.

Only when the puppy has learned to quarter the ground adequately up to a hedge and back again is it wise to start the training as regards jumping gates, or going through fences and hedges. The training however is simplicity itself. All that is required is the firing of a shot in the direction of a low fence or gate and the throwing of a dummy in a realistic fashion by an assistant on the other side. The command 'Hie Lost' is then given and accompanied by the order 'Over'. There should be no difficulty in getting the order obeyed, if a suitable solid fence or gate some three feet high is chosen.

There is always danger that a spirited dog may tear itself on a barbed wire fence through jumping with a heavy hare or bird in its mouth. I like, therefore, teaching a dog to go through a fence as well. This can easily enough be taught by simply standing beside the fence and indicating the means of passage required, with the command 'Through' and a stern 'No' should any other means be attempted.

All these lessons may seem trivial but it must be remembered that the dog's final performance is based on the performance of many such trivial actions. So long as the puppy understands its lessons thoroughly so far, no undue time should be spent in practising them. The time has come to press on to the real thing. There remains but one major step before the practice should start in earnest over game shot in the field.

The puppy is now ranging and quartering the ground reasonably well. It will drop to command, signal, shot, whistle and game flushed. It will scent and point game rigidly and flush at command, and then drop. It will retrieve the dummy under natural conditions with all the distractions and trying circumstances of field work emulated as nearly as possible.

Now the time has come when the puppy must be taught to retrieve dead game and to follow the trail of wounded game. It must learn to distinguish between the trail of wounded game and untouched game. It must learn to cast round when scent appears to have failed and it must learn above all to rely on its nose and not on vision.

It is in this next stage of training that the trainer himself, however blasé he may be, will seldom fail to enjoy a thrill of satisfaction as he watches his puppy puzzle out a long and difficult laid trail to carry out a triumphant retrieve. For it is in this stage that the coping stone is laid to the puppy's training for a useful career as a gundog. The advanced lesson has been reached and the puppy now graduates from the novice to the finished article. It is but one step from learning to follow a laid trail effectively to carrying out a really spectacular retrieve on a strong runner in the shooting field, which is a thing that can surely never fail to gladden the heart of any handler.

SIX

Advanced Training

THE YOUNGSTER is now nearly ready for the shooting field. There would probably be little harm done by shooting over him at this juncture, but the fact remains that there are still some important points for him to learn. Nor is it suggested that his education is complete when he first takes the field in earnest. Although the basic essentials can be learned beforehand much of the field craft and knowledge of field work that are desirable can only be learned in action out shooting.

It is certainly not desirable to keep the dog permanently on dummies and practice work with a view to using him only at Field Trials. Such practices are likely to rebound deservedly on those foolish enough to be parties to them. The dog will probably become thoroughly bored and refuse to work at all adequately. On the other hand it is not advisable to work the young dog too soon.

It must often have been observed how a young dog in its first season, having come upon the hot scent of a runner, and having followed it to a successful conclusion, thereafter never put a foot wrong. Such a dog, of course, had a considerable advantage over its less fortunate field companions. It learned early that in order to achieve results it had to use its nose effectively. Without such a lesson the average dog has to learn this the hard way by trial and error however much basic instinct he may have. It might

even, if successful in one or two retrieves by eye, develop
the bad habit of working by eye alone, running round in
wild circles in the hope of finding its quarry instead of
using its nose.

Rather than chance the puppy learning bad habits, the
obvious thing to do is to teach it to use its nose by the
simple method of laying a trail for it to follow, emulating
the shooting field as nearly as possible. Inevitably the
puppy that has been taught in this fashion will prove a
more useful retriever in the working days that lie ahead of
it. Also it is in the laying of the trail and watching the
puppy following it that the trainer himself learns much
about his dog. He will see the speed and ability with
which it can follow a scent and he will be able to watch
how it faces up to and surmounts the difficulties it
encounters in the task. If he has not already done so he
will begin to assess accurately his dog's qualities.

Prior to the laying of the trail the puppy should be
introduced to the retrieve of game in place of the dummy
it has been accustomed to hitherto. A duck is probably
best to start with, being a close-feathered bird not easily
harmed. With the wings and head tucked firmly into a
piece of old inner tubing round the body it makes a neat
compact mouthful to retrieve. In this way the puppy
learns the correct way to hold game without any danger
of damaging it and learning bad habits. Some people
believe in first adding artificial wings to the dummy but I
do not feel this is really necessary so long as the early
game retrieved is bound in the fashion described.

It is important to remember that only freshly shot game
be used and care must be taken that it is not badly shot
or bloody. Any game in this state, or conversely anything
with a whiff of corruption, or anything that is cold and
stiff, may lead to mouthing or refusal to retrieve, if not
worse. At this stage even more than earlier it is important

Dizzying pigeons by rocking gently with head under wing and laying n back. Note twig used as marker.

Bringing youngster on point under control. Stroke gently to show appreciation. Same dizzied pigeon as previous photograph.

Early lesson in flushing game. Dizzied pigeon.

Point on fur. Hind leg raised.

The point may be made with head high or low.

Game flushed, the youngster drops and marks fall.

Lesson in steadiness. Handler retrieves while youngster is left behind.

that nothing should go wrong. For similar reasons therefore it is advisable not to use the same bird more than once. Once practice loses reality it tends to degenerate into mere routine. For this reason, as progress is made, so the lessons must be constantly varied. However, it is not my suggestion that this part of the training should be protracted in any way. Once the puppy has followed one or two laid trails successfully it is time to continue the training in the shooting field itself.

There are several methods of laying a trail for the young dog to follow. The most important point to realise is that you can't just lay it with a piece of string attached to the dead game. I have seen this done and the dog ignore the game laid for it at the end of the trail to go on to claim the man who had laid the trail. On one occasion I saw a classic example of this. A sack of rabbits was being carried by a helper for use as dead game on a retrieving test. One young dog ignored the rabbit and went straight to the source and claimed the man some fifty yards away. Had I been the judge I would not have penalised that dog, as the method employed was wrong. The dog, in fact, had given a first-class demonstration that its nose was sound and its training weak.

It must be clear from the start, therefore, that the trail has to be laid so that there are no other disturbing scents overlaying it, or close to it. Some people use a tame mallard or pheasant with clipped wings to lay the trail. A pigeon is not much use for the purpose, being too slow a walker. Another method is to lay a piece of string some fifty to a hundred yards long on the chosen ground and leave it out for forty-eight hours or more until all scent has disappeared and then attach the game to one end of it and pull it in.

The disadvantage of both these methods is that no breaks can be introduced in the trail to simulate reality

F

and in the latter case the trail is of necessity almost straight. Also I do not think it wise to teach the puppy to follow the scent of unwounded game. Nor on the other hand do I approve of the method of nicking the leg of a rabbit and letting it go to leave a blood trail. Quite apart from humane considerations there is insufficient control over the trail and it may prove too difficult for the young dog. It is important that the dog should be successful in order to encourage him.

The soundest and in many ways the simplest method, as I see it, is to attach two pieces of string, or binder twine, each about fifty yards long to a freshly shot bird. The trainer and the assistant then each take an end. When the strings are taut and the bird is off the ground it may be carried to the place where it is desired to start the trail. The trail may then be laid with zig-zags and breaks to simulate the real thing. It is advisable, however, not to make it too hard to start with in case the young dog is defeated. At the end of the trail another freshly shot bird is thrown to the desired spot where the somewhat battered towed bird is lifted. Of course the towed bird must be carried well clear of the end of the trail before being lowered to the ground and removed. The trail is then to all intents and purposes exactly like the fresh trail of a runner. There are no overlaying or crossing scents to sidetrack the dog and there is a freshly killed bird at the end of it.

To carry out this method successfully a brace of birds should first be shot. Partridges or grouse are ideal. The fact that they have already been retrieved by another dog will not matter, but it is preferable to avoid even this if possible. The trainer and his assistant must then quickly lay the trail as described, leaving the fresh undamaged bird at the end of it. The trainer then brings up the puppy and the assistant throws a dummy from a concealed position so that it may be seen in the air but lands out of sight of the puppy at apparently somewhere near the start of the trail. The trainer greets the dummy with a shot and then casts the puppy on to the start of the trail with the command 'Hie Lost'. The stage management of the start is therefore as nearly as possible approximating to the shooting field.

A further refinement which may be added to instil a valuable lesson is the throwing of a second dummy a moment after the first which is also greeted with a shot. The second bird or dummy, however, is left lying in the open for the puppy to see easily. Should the puppy attempt to go for it, it must be redirected with a firm 'No' and a wave of the hand in the direction of the other. In this way the puppy soon learns to leave dead game and search for the runner. At the same time the always important lesson is driven home yet again that the trainer's decision on what shall be retrieved is law. Every occasion to instil this steadiness in training and in practice should be taken.

This may sound to some people as if it is superfluous. There is always the man who is ready to assure you that his dog worked perfectly without all this preparation. The fact remains that there is very little trouble involved and anyone can manage quite easily to contrive a near approach to the shooting field such as has been described. I am certain that if they do so and take that little extra trouble with their dog's training they will be more than amply repaid time and time again, both in game saved for the bag and in tempers saved for another day. There is nothing more satisfying out shooting than to see your dog carry out a difficult retrieve after pointing and flushing the game perfectly and, after only one such exhibition faultlessly executed, the average man's shooting day is made.

After one or two successful retrieves on a laid trail the subsequent training should take place in the shooting field itself. The commands that have been taught so far include 'No', 'Sit', 'Heel', 'Cast On', 'Hie Lost', 'Steady', 'Up', 'Over', 'Through' and hand signals. The young dog can now quarter the ground to hand signals and whistle, he can point staunchly and flush to command, he is steady to game flushed and shot, and he can carry out a difficult retrieve to hand. All this without any game being killed over him. In short his training as a novice is over and his training proper has begun.

It is advisable, however, once the dog has begun to retrieve game to accustom it by degrees to retrieving all the different types of game it is likely to encounter. A crow is often a useful means of encouraging the youngster to retrieve strange and unpleasant-tasting objects. Starlings, too, are an unpleasant mouthful and if the dog can be encouraged to retrieve them it will probably retrieve woodcock later on, for, as is well known, they also have a scent peculiarly unpleasing to many dogs resulting in refusal to retrieve them. Although it may be tempting to do so it is not advisable to resort to the method of the forced retrieve in cases of refusal. It is better by far to ignore a temporary refusal to retrieve an evil-tasting object. Once the dog has savoured the pleasures of field work and understands what is expected of it, it is far less likely to refuse. Encouragement and careful training are always preferable to the use of force.

One of the first things the trainer must realise is that if he wishes his dog to give a really polished performance it is wise for him to take it steadily to begin with. Many a dog has been spoiled after a slow and careful training through being rushed in the first days in the shooting field, before it has fully grasped all that is going on around it. Undue interference should be avoided. As far as possible the youngster should be allowed to learn for itself. From now on it should be becoming increasingly a partner in the proceedings. The handler should remember that its scenting powers are superior to his and unwarranted interference in early retrieves can often result in the puppy merely returning to the handler on the heel scent.

At the same time it is essential at this stage that the youngster should have the full and undivided support of its trainer. It is, therefore, a wise precaution that the trainer should devote himself for the first few outings exclusively to handling his dog and leave the shooting to his assistant or to other trusted shots. The sport that is lost thereby will be more than amply repaid in the years to come, but it is probable anyway that the trainer will find that in watching his own pupil working at last he has reward enough.

The first stage is probably teaching the young dog to hunt methodically in cover. To begin with a suitable small patch of gorse or similar cover may be chosen and the dog encouraged to enter it. The trainer must now work the dog through it methodically, discouraging any attempt to leave it until it has been thoroughly hunted. On any game being flushed the command 'Up' should be given and the dog stopped from pursuing it from the cover. In practice the dog should very quickly get the idea of what is required.

The next step is probably teaching the young dog to work a hedge or ditch, staying within reasonable range of the handler. In the same way he must learn not to range too far out in thick cover. To begin with this may all require a certain amount of verbal encouragement, before the dog fully understands what is required of him. It will be readily appreciated that if the trainer has to handle a gun and keep half his attention on the shooting,

he cannot help or control his dog in the same way as if
he is unencumbered. However, if care is taken in these
early stages, it should not be long before the dog fully
understands what is required of it. If it is felt necessary
artificially introduced substitutes for wild game may be
used to drive these lessons home.

At this stage of training comes what is perhaps the
greatest thrill of all. The practice of what the Germans
term the 'Umschlagen', or, literally, 'Strike round'. This
encircling movement is encouraged in their general
purpose Pointer-Retrievers and is akin to the curve of the
Setter or Pointer. While normally the dog will hold the
game fixed with its point until the arrival of the handler
and the order to flush, there are times later on in the
season, as the game gets wilder, when a wily old cock
pheasant or Frenchman will run ahead. It is in order to
hold these birds fixed that this movement is encouraged
and it is fascinating to watch the battle of wits between a
wise dog and a crafty old bird.

For the first attempt at this movement it is desirable to
have certain conditions. The dog should have come on
point in the middle of a field or large open space, where
there is sufficient ground cover to allow the game to run
unobserved. If, as the trainer approaches, the dog
advances stealthily in a crouched point, so much the better.
This drawing on means almost certainly that the game is
running ahead.

This is the moment to attract the dog's attention with
a vigorous hand signal to the right, or left, according to the
direction of the wind, and another vigorous hand signal
forward. Verbal encouragement may have to be added,
as this is, after all, contrary to all previous teaching:
however, as the game is running ahead anyway, this will
probably not matter. If the dog's hunting instincts are
highly developed it is quite possible that it will grasp the

idea at once. Of course, on the other hand, it is possible that a dog will never achieve complete perfection in this movement and it must be stressed that it should only be attempted when the dog has been already fully trained in every other way and is already a staunch pointer; possibly not until the second season. Otherwise not only is it unlikely to be successful but, being contrary to previous training, it is likely to cause confusion in the dog's mind and a serious setback in training.

It is impossible, however, to do justice verbally to the way an experienced dog performs this movement. He should break away at an angle to the game with a smooth drop of the shoulder and advance with a fluid movement, belly almost to the ground. Somehow, while keeping his body low to the ground and taking full advantage of the cover he must keep his muzzle high and towards the game, without losing contact at any time. As a feat of stalking it is well worth watching.

With a fast-moving cock it is not always that the complete encircling movement is possible. Usually in such a case the dog will manage to move in and hold it fixed from the side. The real climax, however, comes when the encircling movement is completed and there is the dog facing the handler on staunch point with the bird or covey held in between them ready to be flushed at the command or signal. That to me is the height of dog work.

These, however, are the highlights of this advanced training in the field. Every opportunity should be taken in the first season to accustom the young dog to novel experiences and to give him the chance to improve his own education. If driven shooting is available he should be taken out with the beaters on a drive and practise his work there. He should be made to sit behind the guns steadily and practise what he has learned in steadiness and retrieving. He must learn to distinguish each

different type of game and to retrieve them all. He must
be taken wild-fowling and given a chance to retrieve the
ducks in his other element. All the while his trainer must
be prepared to help him to the full, if necessary not
himself shooting while doing so. For the month or so that
may be missed he should have many enjoyable years
companionship and partnership to make up for it.

This is not to say, however, I repeat, at danger of being
monotonous, that the training should ever be regarded as
finished. There is always something still to learn. Nor
should it necessarily be the dog who is learning. Each day
out with the gun should reveal something fresh that has
not been noted before. If only the handler gets into the
habit of watching the dog all the time he will soon begin
to notice much that has escaped him previously. That
movement of the head as the dog quartered there meant
that a hare's form lay warm in the stubble, the occupant
but lately gone and the mud still bearing his imprint.
That faint pause there meant that he caught wind of a
covey of partridges that moved out as you entered the
field.

As the dog works, so the handler should be interpreting
each movement of tail and head, each pause and hesitation. All should convey their message to the handler so
that he can work out what lies ahead of them. However,
to begin with, the handler who is new to the idea will
probably see little difference in the speedy movement of
the dog's quartering and the suddenness of the point will
catch him unawares.

It must be remembered that shooting with a dog in
front in this way is entirely different from simply walking
up game. An element of hunting has entered into it.
Whyte Melville wrote "There is no greater treat to a
lover of the chase than to watch a pack of high-bred fox
hounds that have been running hard on pasture brought

suddenly to a check on the dusty sun dried fallows. They will literally quarter their ground like pointers, till they recover the line . . ."

To see the dog using the wind, to watch it scenting with head held high one moment and low the next, to watch it race on a scent breast-high, or work a ticklish scent at nearly comparable speed, that is all hound work. To use the wind correctly, to interpret the signs the dog makes, invisible to the unknowledgeable, as correctly as the handler's signs must be interpreted by the dog, that is all hunting.

The dog must become an extension of the man himself; an extra sense; a partner on four legs. That partnership must be working together in communion and harmony of thought and action and each half of the partnership must pull his weight equally: it being always borne in mind that, nine times out of ten, the human partner is the less effective working unit.

Once the handler has reached this stage of under-standing, he and his dog should enjoy every outing to the full. For there is something special about any dog that hunts in conjunction with its handler. Anyone who has owned a dog trained in this way will appreciate this quotation from "The Master of Game" by Edward, Duke of York, circa 1410:

"A hound is of great understanding and of great knowledge, a hound hath great strength and great good-ness, a hound is a wise beast and a kind (one). A hound has a great memory and great smelling, a hound has great diligence and great might, a hound is of great worthiness and of great subtlety, a hound is of great lightness and of great perception, a hound is of good obedience, for he will learn as a man all that a man will teach him. A hound is full of good sport."

SEVEN

Brace Work and Trials

I T MUST be made clear to begin with that two general purpose Pointer-Retrievers are not necessarily better than one. Effectively trained and handled a suitable working dog should be more than able to fulfil expectations. Certainly one dog working well is infinitely preferable to two dogs working indifferently and, if one of a pair is working badly, it is almost certain to affect the other, for there is nothing more infectious than a bad example being set by another dog. At the same time there is a certain unique satisfaction to be felt in watching a well balanced, well matched pair of dogs working together as a team.

It is desirable, if two dogs are being used together, to have them paired for ages, size, temperament and work as far as possible. This is not just a matter of appearance. It must be appreciated that a young, fast, large dog will probably not work satisfactorily with an old, slow, small dog. Apart from physical differences their methods of working must almost certainly be diametrically opposed to each other. True an old dog may sometimes serve to steady a wild young dog, but that is a very different matter from pairing dogs that are almost complementary to each other in their work, i.e. one short range Pointer-Retriever and one long range Pointer-Retriever together, instead of a balanced pair. Almost inevitably any young dog set to work with an old dog will develop according to the example the old dog sets, whether it is good or bad, and if the old dog is not thoroughly reliable it will have an unsettling effect on both of them.

There is far more to the adequate working of two dogs together, however, than just taking two matched dogs out in the shooting field. If they are trained dogs used to working alone they may not take kindly to working as part of a team. Apart from a refusal to back or honour the other's points, jealousy may easily arise, causing unsteadiness and disobedience. Since there is always the possibility that your dog may meet another general-purpose Pointer-Retriever in the shooting field however it is advisable to accustom every dog to brace work, so that they can be worked in front in company with another dog if required. This should be part of every general-purpose dog's education.

If a pair of dogs are to be worked by one handler, however, the ideal is to have two well matched, well trained dogs. They must be capable of understanding when a command is addressed to them by name and ignore any commands that are not. Hence the importance of short working names which must be clear and distinct. It is also, of course, vital that both dogs' primary obedience training is sound. If one dog runs in you can scarcely blame the other for following suit. So that, though it is sometimes a sound practice to use a well trained dog to steady a younger, over-exuberant dog, it is not usually advisable to work a partially trained dog in company with another. It is up to the trainer to judge from his experience and knowledge of the dogs concerned whether they will work together well or not. Some people are great believers in setting an old dog to teach a younger one, but my own feeling is that it is usually wiser to let the young dog develop on its own and learn its own way. As in everything else, this must depend on the dogs, the trainer and the circumstances.

Given a pair of dogs well matched in temperament, size and ability and accustomed to working together, there are few things more pleasing to the eye. They will follow docilely to heel in a mannered fashion, with no running ahead to enter a field in front of the handler, and they will drop individually or together at command or signal. When it is desired that they should start working the ground, they should each be dropped and then sent off in turn with the command and wave of the hand. How they work must depend on the nature of the ground. If the ground is restricted they may be expected to cross in front of the handler like a brace of pointers, each quartering roughly the same area in front of the handler. If the ground is rough, with thick cover, they may be required to work close in front, each making good his own ground in front of the handler, barely crossing each other's ground. If the ground is open and flat they may be expected to range wide, each covering their own area and barely crossing once more. How they work must always depend on the ground and the handler's requirements and on the build and temperament of the dogs themselves.

As soon as one dog comes on point, however, the other must honour that point by backing (coming on point also at a distance). The game should then be flushed by the dog which first came on point and both dogs should drop. Both dogs may be allowed to road out the scent but the dog that came on point should always be sent to retrieve the game. The other meanwhile remains steady. Then, at the command, each in turn should start quartering the ground once more.

In effect, it must be realised, the range of two dogs is not necessarily greater than that of one. Frequently the very presence of a second dog will curtail the effort that each makes in this respect so that sometimes the ground covered is no greater than if there were only one working. Once again, however, range must basically be dependent on the ground. It is also one of the most important rules of handling that both dogs must be in sight the whole time.

The range itself is unlikely to be greater than eighty or a hundred yards to either side of the handler and some forty or so in front. This forms about the maximum size of quadrilateral inside which it is feasible for the dogs to work at the pace of the average man's advance. If they are to increase their pace it is only likely to be at risk of missing game. The same rule must hold good if they are expected to cover any greater amount of ground. In practice the area covered will almost always be a good deal less than this, dependent as ever on the ground.

It will be appreciated, however, that the standard of control which must be exercised by the handler over two dogs is considerably higher than over one. The effort of concentration required to maintain perfect control over both dogs, unless both are old hands together, is extremely high and to my mind precludes shooting at the same time. Only when the dogs have been well accustomed to working together with the handler can he afford to allow his attention to relax.

It must also be obvious that the puppy or young dog has some more lessons coming to him in this respect before he can be adjudged a fully trained dog. In actual fact, if the young dog has already been fully trained on his own, which is the method I would always advocate, he has not a great deal to learn. He must learn to work independently of the other dog working with him. He must learn to back and honour the other's points. He must learn to drop as the other dog flushes the game and to stay down while the other dog goes on to retrieve.

As I see it the best time to start this brace-work training

is when the dog has been through the entire course of training so far suggested by himself, as puppies training together may always develop at different speeds. I do not think it is a sound idea to train the puppy to work in conjunction with an older dog to start with as this is inclined to sap its initiative and drive. It is admittedly quite often a sound plan to use an old and fully trained dog to set the puppy an example in the early days, i.e. in walking to heel, or retrieving, but this is quite a different matter from early training in brace work. Especially is this to be noted in the matter of pointing. Although the old dog may be used to find the location of wild game, I do not advise that the puppy should be shown the older dog pointing and taught by its example, being led round on a check lead while the other quarters. This is the sort of thing that tends to make the puppy reliant on others to do the work and leads to blinking, if not worse.

The first step of all is to ensure that the young dog does not shadow the other. At the first sign of this tendency the young dog must be dropped and the other allowed to quarter well clear before the young dog is allowed to continue. This will only have to be done a few times to make the young dog appreciate that his mind must be kept on the job.

More difficult to cure is a refusal to honour the other's points and back properly. The most heinous crime here, of course, is pressing in front of the dog already on point or stealing the point. In practice if the young dog is a sound pointer he will almost certainly back instinctively. It may be that he will catch the scent from another angle and come on point from another side. This, however, if not actually backing, is at least honouring the point.

It is sometimes hard to say whether a dog has actually seen the other's point or not. In this respect jealousy amongst kennel companions can have surprising results.

I have seen one dog consistently ignore another's points yet out with another dog he would back him without fail. It is important to remember that undue attention to one or other of a pair can easily breed this sort of jealousy. For this very reason the dog that has made the point must always be rewarded with the retrieve. If the retrieve is consistently given to the other dog the first dog will easily be soured. He might even cease working efficiently as a direct result.

Should the young dog persistently refuse to back the other, it must be dropped by command and brought up slowly into position, if necessary on the check lead. Should it persistently attempt to pass the other dog, it must be checked with the command 'No' and again, if necessary the check lead. If there is any difficulty it might even be necessary to go back to the artificially introduced substitute to wild game.

Last of all, but possibly the hardest test of all, the young dog must learn to remain dropped while the other dog is sent off to retrieve. In fact, as this is simply an advanced test for his obedience training, there should be no great trouble involved once the trainer has cautioned him with a firm 'No' at any attempt to move. Should he attempt to move after the command 'No', drastic measures must be taken and the check lead is again the answer.

Once the young dog has learned to work in harmony with others he can truly be considered well on the way to being a trained dog. The trainer, however, must always have one eye open for any contingencies which might affect his work. Should he be worked too long in the company of an older slower dog, for instance, it may be certain that his own work will be adversely affected. It is surprising how infectious a bad example can be. For this reason the young dog should never be worked in the company of unreliable dogs. Should one of them run in, it may mean that the young dog follows suit with consequent damage to be undone by the trainer. He has certainly learned his lesson well if he can be dropped in the face of such an insidious example.

In practice, when an old dog is being taken out in company with a younger, stronger dog, it is often not either fair or sensible that they should be matched against each other. The most equable way of using them then might be to work the old dog for a while until he begins to tire and keep the other to heel in the meantime. Then at a suitable moment they might be changed round and the old dog kept in to heel while the youngster goes through its paces.

It will probably have been gathered that most owners will be more than satisfied with one dog and only the enthusiast will aim at using two or more. On the other hand most people, once they have trained a dog in this way, become enthusiasts. It is, in fact, likely that the roughshooter who has once trained a dog to the stage that has been suggested will never want to change his method of shooting. He will probably find that he is enjoying each day's sport more than he would in the past have believed possible. If his youngster is working really well, he may even be thinking seriously in terms of Field Trials.

In this country there is no equivalent of the so called 'Meat Dog' Trials which are held in the United States and elsewhere. These are in effect Pointer-Retriever Trials open to any breed. The dogs are expected to find game, point, back and retrieve. In other words to act as a general purpose Pointer-Retriever.

The normal method of working these Trials is that the dogs are drawn in pairs. Each pair is taken in turn in front of the judge and worked over suitable ground by their respective handlers. Game is pointed, shot and retrieved as it would be under normal working con-

dvanced training. A crow is a useful means of encouraging
oungster to retrieve unpleasant tasting objects.

Steady on point.

Honouring flush. Dropping to flushed game.

ditions. A gun accompanies each handler, although it may be optional for the handler to carry a gun himself.

The judge marks for ranging and quartering, for game-finding ability, pointing, backing, behaviour at flushed game and general style. He also marks for the standard of control between handler and dog and for retrieving ability. Apart from this they may be tested for cover work and work in water.

There are several different systems used for marking and judging such Trials, but whichever system is used it will be appreciated that the judge has a very formidable task in front of him. In effect he has to assess the working ability, keeness and enthusiasm of each dog and weigh the imponderables of scent and scenting quickly and decide eventually in favour of an individual dog. Considering the difficult task which often faces the specialist Field Trial judge, it will be appreciated that judging such a Trial is no easy matter.

Of course there is nothing to stop the dog of a retriever breed, which has been trained in the manner suggested, from being entered in a Retriever Field Trial. Similarly a dog of a Pointer or Setter breed, trained in the same way, might be entered in a Pointer and Setter Trial. If the training has been thoroughly carried out the dog should be capable of performing creditably.

As there are usually novice and puppy stakes, as well as open stakes, in any sort of Field Trial the average owner stands as good a chance as anyone. In fact it is good training for the dogs to enter them in such an event. They are likely to benefit from an outing during which they learn to conduct themselves in novel conditions. The owners, too, are likely to benefit from an exchange of views and information.

Generally speaking it is worth an owner entering his dog for a Field Trial, if it has reached a sufficient stage of training, simply for the experience both he and it will gain. That does not mean, however, that an owner who is well aware that his dog is not fully trained should enter his dog. This sort of thing is all too often seen in any breed Trials and it is not fair either on the organisers or the other entrants. If a dog is liable to run wild, or is hard-mouthed, or has any obvious faults, however fond the owner may be of it, and however much he may excuse its faults in private, he should not enter it in a public event.

It need scarcely be added that in any type of Field Trials the judge's awards are final, whatever may be thought of them in private. Too often the disappointed competitor forgets that the judge was, after all, in a better position to see what went on than he was. Apart from that it may well be that the judge's views and the competitor's views on what is required may differ. If that is the case the competitor must simply grin and bear it.

Nor should the competitor worry unduly if his dog runs badly and makes a poor showing. Some dogs work well at Field Trials and are natural showmen themselves. Other dogs will never run well in public. Each dog must vary and the dog that does abominably one day may well be the winner at the next event, or the better dog in practice in the field. Such matters are all in the luck of the game and it is worth persevering if your dog shows sound ability. In practice, however, the average roughshooter will probably be quite contented if his dog works well in the shooting field and satisfies his requirements there.

EIGHT

General Remarks on the Use of the Dogs and Training

C ARE HAS been taken in this book to suggest words of command which are not liable to cause confusion in the dog's mind and to keep them to the bare minimum. The only ones out of the ordinary are 'Cast On', instead of the more usual 'Hold Up', which might be confused with the command for flushing game, and the use of 'No', instead of the more common 'Toho' or 'Hoe', as a steadying influence on point. Also, as far as possible, the order of training has been given both logically and chronologically, each lesson being kept separate and distinct.

In practice, however, anyone training a dog on the lines indicated will find that it is often impossible to have any clear-cut distinction between one stage of training and the next. This almost inevitable overlapping between various stages of training is not a thing to worry about unduly so long as there is no danger of confusion in the dog's mind. Nor should the amateur trainer worry if he does not spend as much time with his dog as he would like. Two half-hourly periods of training in the day should be enough and most people can spare the time for that. The dangers of overdoing the training have been sufficiently stressed not to need repetition. It will be found that an intelligent puppy requires remarkably little

training, if that training is conducted on the right
lines.

It is only when the puppy has not been taught primary
obedience, or has been mishandled, that its training is
likely to be a lengthy and protracted business. Hence the
importance, if the puppy is kept in the house, not so
much of training the puppy, as training the household.
Given a systematic, even if brief, training on the lines
suggested, the puppy should develop into a useful shooting
partner.

Anyone who has read this suggested course of training
so far will have a fairly clear idea of how the dog should
be worked in practice. From their experiences in training
their puppy most people will have decided for themselves
what is correct as regards range and pace for their dog.
As it has been stressed from the beginning that the
dog should be a variable-range, variable-pace Pointer-
Retriever it is obviously impossible to give any hard and
fast ruling. The fact remains, however, that if the dog is
ranging at more than a hundred yards to either side and
forty yards in front it is likely to be moving at a speed
which makes it very liable to miss game.

It is not easy to imagine a quadrilateral in front of
the handler approximately 200 yards by 40 yards, but if
anyone is still in doubt about this I advise him to pace out
a field and divide it into marked quadrilaterals inside
which he can watch his dog working. A few markers are
all that is needed and, if he places some pigeons or other
artificially introduced substitutes for wild game on the
ground, he will be able to ensure that his dog is not
missing any game.

If the dog is working as a matter of course outside the
limits suggested then it is more than probable it will be
missing game. It is barely possible for a dog of average
ability to do otherwise. In practice, however, the average

handler will probably be content to range the dog at fifty to sixty yards either side most of the time. This is ample for most purposes in rough shooting.

Certainly, whatever distance the dog is ranging must be governed by the animal's ability (pace and nose), the nature of the ground and scenting conditions. The first two of these the handler may think he knows well enough, but it is a bold man, even on his own ground, who can forecast scenting conditions accurately. Often when conditions appear good they turn out to be bad and, conversely, it sometimes happens that when conditions appear bad it is soon obvious that they are nothing of the sort.

There is really only one reliable guide to scenting conditions and that is the behaviour of the dog. The handler will learn very quickly that he can and must trust his dog completely. There should be little question with the well trained dog of doing more than indicating the general lines on which it is desired to work. The dog with its superior powers of scenting to guide it should automatically cover the ground effectively and adjust its pace to the scenting conditions. It therefore follows that the pace must always be variable when working a dog in this way and it is a sine qua non that the range must be variable with the pace, just as the reverse is true. Both range and pace are in fact governed to a considerable extent by the dog and its ability as well as the nature of the ground. The handler with a good dog well trained may always rely on it.

In this connection no one should ever be ashamed to admit that they have learned from their dog, at any stage of its training. In fact both handler and dog should be learning from each other all the time. Especially is this true in the case of the novice in field work. Whole new worlds should be opening up in front of him each time he goes out with his dog. He will begin to notice the game moving in front of him.

Through his dog he will notice where and how that cock pheasant disappeared and how that covey of partridges moved to one side after flying over the hedge. He will see the hare lying in its form and the rabbit in its tuft of grass. He will learn to pierce Nature's camouflage and see the game around him. As an almost automatic result his interest will be stimulated to the degree where shooting ceases to be of prior importance. The dog's work itself will begin to absorb him increasingly and he will become interested in the preservation of game as well as the study of wild life. In sport it is very true that one thing leads to another.

By trial and error he will learn to use the wind correctly. It is obviously small use having a brilliant dog if a strong wind is blowing from behind and the dog is forty paces or more in front of the handler. Even in these circumstances the dog may succeed in doing his work, but it is handicapping him needlessly. It is small blame to him if game is flushed in the process, or if most of it runs ahead.

There have been many arguments about the scenting abilities of game and some maintain stoutly that game birds cannot scent, but have magnificent hearing and eyesight. It scarcely matters which is correct as there are still plenty of animals which can scent your advance and their flight or alarm call will alert others. That is the law of the wild. Also, wind carries sound as well as scent. It is better to accept the fact that your dog needs the wind to carry the scent to him and that it muffles, by that much, the sound of your approach.

I know of people who always walk up snipe with the wind because they maintain that the snipe always get up into the wind and fly straight towards them for an instant, before turning and twisting. But that implies

that they know where the snipe are to begin with and that
they are capable of hitting them in that instant at a long
range. I prefer to use a general-purpose Pointer-Retriever
with the wind in my face, secure in the knowledge that I
am not missing any snipe, or other game, that may be
lying tight.

It is, however, naturally not always possible to work
with wind ahead. There are times when the ground
dictates that the wind must be to one side or the other, or
from behind. In such cases the handler must take into
consideration where and how he wants his dog to work.
He may continue to work him in front, or he may bring
him in closer, or work him only to one side, or bring him
in to heel.

As the handler becomes accustomed to his dog being in
front, however, he will probably find the thought of
bringing him in to heel more and more abhorrent to him.
It becomes natural to see the dog working in front as an
extension of the handler himself. To bring him in is to
curb the chances of finding game, but naturally there are
occasions when it is the only course.

If the wind is coming strongly from one side the best
method is often to quarter the dog on the other side so
that any game between you and the dog is scented. If
the wind is strongly from behind there is little alternative
but to range the dog within gun shot. In thick cover or
roots, of course, the same procedure must be adopted,
for it is not always the dog's fault if game is flushed without
warning in these circumstances, and if game is to be
flushed without warning it is clearly preferable to have it
flushed within range of shot.

It should generally be regarded as indicative of a fault
in handling if game is flushed without warning being
given of its presence and an opportunity gained of shooting
it. Of course there are occasions when game is seen by the

handler and shot. On such occasions the dog must drop
and wait for the order to retrieve as has been shown in the
training methods.   Generally speaking, however, the
handler will find that such occasions are very much in a
minority if he is using his dog correctly. In most instances
he will receive fair warning of any game ahead.

In the matter of working hedges or ditches the method
used must be dependent on the wind. If there are a strong
cross wind and good scenting conditions, it might well not
be necessary to do more than work the dog along the
hedge in front of the handler. Sometimes the dog may be
used to the windward side of the hedge with the handler
on the other. At other times the dog may have to work
the undergrowth of an overgrown hedge or ditch
systematically. It is impossible to do more than indicate
various methods, which must all be dependent on the
ground, the dog and the circumstances. The overall point
to remember is that you must always be able to see the
dog or know his exact whereabouts. If in any doubt,
don't shoot. Better a missed opportunity than a peppered
dog.

This is also an important point to remember when the
dog is being used in front of a line. The first thing is to
make sure that everyone knows what to do when the dog
points. In these enlightened days it is also advisable to
examine your neighbour closely. He may be an excellent
man with a ·75 howitzer, but a damnably dangerous shot
with a twelve-bore. It is sometimes better in such cases to
keep the dog in to heel. However, it is one of the advantages of roughshooting that numbers are limited and
one usually knows the other guns well.

It is on this question of quartering in front of a line that
the importance of hand signals is demonstrated. If the
dog will not flush to hand signals, or command, it means
that the handler has to break line each time the dog

points, unless the game is to be flushed by the gun or guns in front of whom the dog has pointed, which is not really desirable. Control at a distance is therefore important. Some people advocate the use of a different whistle especially for this purpose, but, if you once start this practice, you are liable to end up with a battery of musical instruments like a one-man band. As with everything else to do with training, the simpler the method the better.

There are people I know who go out shooting laden like a Christmas tree with decoys, calls, whistles, cartridge bags, cartridge belts and optimistically large game bags. Excess paraphernalia of this sort should have no part in the outfit of the roughshooter with a general-purpose dog. A cartridge belt, a gun, a whistle and a game bag are all that should be required. I prefer when working my dogs by myself to dispense even with a game bag and to rely on poacher's pockets, but that is a purely personal preference based on the fact that I find a heavy bag unbalances me.

Though normally I carry a lead, attached to my belt, I often make a point of removing the dogs' collars when they are working in cover, or rough ground, as a collar can sometimes catch in a snag and cause trouble. Frequently, too, I dispense with the whistles I carry and rely on a shrill whistle produced between the teeth. It is surprising how effective this can become with practice. All methods of working should be kept as efficient and simple as possible so long as there is real control and understanding between dog and handler and a clear understanding of the principles involved.

A point worth making in this connection is that when game has been flushed it is not always desirable that the dog should road out the scent. Admittedly when a covey has been flushed there are often stray birds which have remained behind. The purpose of allowing the dog to road out is simply to make sure that these birds or other game are not overlooked. Yet it may often be the case that there is obviously no game left and there may be a strong runner to be retrieved. Although in principle the dog should always be put on to road out the scent, it must therefore, be plain that in practice this must depend on the circumstances.

It will be understood that all I am attempting to do in this book is to lay down some general principles for guidance in the use and training of general-purpose Pointer-Retrievers in this country. The application of these principles in this country must of course vary with individuals and their dogs. The application of these principles outside this country must vary with the locality, the individuals, the dogs and the circumstances even more than they will in this country. Methods of shooting and working dogs must vary from place to place with local custom, ground, game and climate.

In a hot climate, where bad scenting conditions are general and cover is often thick and impenetrable, it is often the wisest, and indeed only, course to train the dog to run in to the fall to retrieve, before the wounded game can slip away without trace. There are, in fact, those who stoutly advocate the same policy in this country for the roughshooter. This does not mean, however, that the training programme suggested is unnecessary. The dog can and should still be taught steadiness first. Once the dog has learned sound basic obedience, which will always stand it in good stead, any other methods of training desired may be adopted.

There are two other closely connected points on which there may well be a divergence of opinion. There is a school of thought which maintains that the handler should flush the game for the dog and, once the game has been flushed, that the dog should remain standing rather than drop. In the United States this is generally the custom. The argument in favour of it is that, if the handler flushed the game, he must be in a position to shoot it and, if the dog drops, it is not likely to be able to mark the fall of the game as well as if it remains standing.

It is admittedly easier not to trouble to train your dog to flush game. If difficulty is experienced in doing so it might possibly be advisable to leave this training until the dog is more mature and experienced, but, to my mind, the advantages gained by training the dog to flush game to order from the very beginning are well worth any extra trouble involved. Nor, taken on the lines indicated, should there be any difficulty experienced.

There are certainly times, which every roughshooter must have experienced, when to flush the game for the dog would result in missing a shot. Especially where game is in any sort of cover, it is important that the dog should be taught to flush it. And if the dog is taught to flush game it follows as a natural corollary that he must be taught to drop on doing so. Nor is it necessarily the case that this should affect his ability to mark the fall of the game. In the sitting position the dog has as good a view as standing and he is still dropped and steady. Standing, there is an ever present temptation to run in. If only as an additional lesson in steadiness, it seems to me well worth while teaching the dog to flush the game and drop.

However much local customs may differ, and local conditions of shooting with them, this is still a sound method of training in that it does not do more than channel the natural instincts of the dog in the required directions. By the end of the suggested method of training the handler should have an adaptable and useful shooting companion with none of his natural ardour and initiative cramped. At the same time he should be a mannered dog.

By that I mean he does not rush in front through doorways
and gateways (i.e. break field), or jump up with muddy
paws, or commit the other canine crimes of impulsiveness.
None of these very obvious points have been mentioned
for the simple reason that the command 'No' was given
as a universal prohibition and it is up to each handler to
use it, along with the appropriate commands 'Sit' and
'Heel', when the dog commits any of these annoying
actions.

One point here is worth stressing. There are few things
more annoying than the noisy dog which is constantly
whining or barking. This is usually put down to temperament, or a fault in breeding, but more often than not it is
a fault in handling. Even the dog with an excitable
temperament can be checked with a sharp word and a
caution at the right time. If this is not done and the vice
becomes a habit, it is of course a very different matter. As
a matter of sound practice any sign of such a tendency
should be checked at once.

It cannot be too often stressed how important careful
handling of the youngster is at all times. Nor can it be
emphasised too strongly that it is worth devoting considerable study to the individual temperament of each dog.
What may be a suitable method of training for one dog
may not be effective with another. Indeed, in some cases,
may even have the diametrically opposed effect to that
intended. Thus undue pressure brought to bear on a
sensitive dog might have the effect of souring it completely,
or breaking its spirit, while similar treatment of its more
robust or phlegmatic kennel mate might have little or no
effect.

It has been stressed throughout each phase of training
how the wrong approach may cause resistances to the
training to be set up and how with each dog the approach
must differ. A distinction must always be borne in mind,

however, between the young dog and the old offender. The old offender is one who has been badly or carelessly handled for several seasons. When a dog has once developed bad habits, such as running into shot, or alternatively what a Head Keeper friend of mine aptly calls 'closing the suitcase', probably through being put on to retrieving large and still lively hares, he is difficult, if not impossible, to cure. Prevention is always better and easier than cure in such cases.

Admittedly drastic cases sometimes seem to call for drastic cures, but patience, perseverance and simplicity should always be the keynotes of training. There should never be any attempts at short cuts in training. They very seldom, if ever, pay. Usually they merely result in more work in the long run and the same may generally be said of the many varied and ingenious devices which are so often suggested.

It never ceases to surprise me how many people seem to place their faith in tricks such as placing a shot pigeon in an old nylon stocking to encourage the youngster to retrieve game. And, of course, there are the hoary old chestnuts about sewing a hedgehog inside a rabbit skin, or a piece of 'Monkey Puzzle' inside a sock dummy, for the youngster who shows a tendency towards hard mouth. Also there are always the inevitable old hands at 'dog breaking' who talk glibly of dummies stuffed with barbed wire, or tying a rabbit in the mouth of the dog with a propensity for chewing game. If any such methods ever worked, it is probable that it was only in individual cases where more normal methods with patience would have worked as well. Such kill-or-cure methods may work occasionally, but it is doubtful if the results would be as permanent as careful and patient training would achieve, nor is there ever any excuse for trying them on a young dog.

With an old and hardened offender, little in the way of punishment or attempted cure is likely to have much permanent effect. That any dog should become an incorrigible is, however, a reflection on its handler. It must always be borne in mind, and cannot be over-emphasised, that the training of dog and handler is never finished. On every outing the handler should be alert to prevent any sign of incipient misbehaviour as well as taking every opportunity to drive any needed lesson home. In this way both dog and handler should be constantly learning from each other.

It is always worth persevering, for even a season or more, until the youngster has been given every chance to grow out of a bad habit, although, of course, that is not to say that any bad habit should ever be either condoned or allowed to pass unchecked. The puppy must always be checked, but, rather than try a drastic cure, it is usually worth letting some time pass and gentler methods have every chance of success first.

The old days of dog breaking, rather than training, have passed, but in one other important respect gundog training has altered radically. The absence of rabbits due to myxomatosis, whether permanent or not, has altered gundog training methods, as it has altered our shooting habits, considerably. In one way it has made specialist training easier and in another way more difficult. It is no longer necessary, or, in many cases, possible, to teach the command 'Ware Rabbit'. It is doubtful, however, if this could ever have been considered a command used by the roughshooter.

Even should the rabbit return in limited numbers, as I am convinced it will in spite of extermination orders, there is no reason why the method of training advocated should in any way be altered. Training on fur can be carried out on hares on the lines indicated, always presuming them to be available, and any rabbits seen may be pointed, flushed and shot in the same way. If required, the intelligent dog, sensibly handled, could be checked from showing an interest in rabbits, just as he can be checked from showing an undue interest in larks, or cheepers, with the command 'No'. In practice, however, the average roughshooter will usually be only too pleased to have a healthy rabbit as a useful addition to the gamebag.

NINE

A Full Bag

LOOKING BACK over the pages of the game book there are many days that stand out in the memory for one reason or another. For the pure pleasure of the day as well as the satisfying bag I found my mind lingering when I reached November 2nd, 1951. That was certainly one of those red-letter days as far as satisfaction and sport are concerned. The weather was perfect, the dog worked splendidly and my shooting was above average. Surely the perfect combination to make a memorable day.

We started out, Max and I, with a full cartridge belt and an empty game bag at ten o'clock in the morning and we came back at four well laden. But I am anticipating. When we started out we were merely aware that the air was tingling with freshness and the sun pleasantly warm and not too bright. Altogether it was one of those fresh late Autumn days when it is good to be alive and in the open country with a gun and a dog. Obviously Max felt much the same for he was making occasional little whining noises in his throat and wagging his tail to show what he thought about it.

When we entered the first stubble field and started to walk it up into the wind, he was off like a flash at my signal. Almost at once, before he was fully into his stride, he froze rigidly with his neck at an angle to his body in a curiously twisted way. In a few strides I was up on him

slipping cartridges into my gun as I went. The sharp
click as I snapped the breech was enough to flush the
covey that he was holding pinned down and, with a
startled whirr, they were off.

I still had plenty of time for a right and left and it was
an augury of the day to come that two plump birds were
lying dead in the stubble a moment later. Max, who had
gone down automatically as he always does when the
birds were flushed, looked up eagerly for the command to
retrieve and it seemed to me looked a little disgusted when
I performed the job myself.

A few moments later, however, he was off again
quartering the ground with that tireless stride of his
which looks so deceptive and yet covers the ground so
speedily. Again he had barely covered fifty yards before
he froze, this time into a straightforward point, tail, nose
and back straight and near hind leg lifted. This time I
was able to give the command 'Up' and a fine buck hare
was flushed from its form. I made no mistake about it and
a moment later it was turning a cartwheel shot through
the head. Once more in spite of Max's reproachful look I
retrieved it myself.

It looked like being a good day and no mistake now.
Scarcely five minutes gone and a brace of partridges and
a big eight-pound hare in the bag. But there were better
things to come. Hardly had Max started quartering
again than he froze once more. Again on the command
'Up' he flushed a hare, the mate of the first. Again shot
through the head, it cartwheeled to a standstill. This
looked like becoming almost too much of a good thing.
At this rate I was going to be overloaded in next to no
time.

I decided to drop the game at the corner of the field
and return for it later. I was in two minds about leaving
the bag as well, but for once I decided against doing so.

Normally I dislike carrying a bag as, having a game leg, I find it tends to unbalance me. Unless I am out for a full day I prefer to rely on my 'poacher's pockets'. As it was, prudence told me that my present haul was quite likely to be the sum total of the bag but optimism was undaunted. With a start like this in the very first field it was bound to be a good day. Nor, for once, was my optimism misplaced.

At the very moment I was leaving the hares and the brace of partridges in a safe spot in the hedge, I saw Max pointing firmly at a tussock of grass. His hind leg was up again so it looked like a hare or a rabbit. I dropped the game bag on the spot and went to investigate. At my approach a fine healthy rabbit bounded out and was cleanly dispatched with the right barrel. A brace of partridges, two hares and a rabbit inside the first half hour. Oh! what a beautiful morning. My spirits soared even higher. This was going to be a good day, I felt sure now.

With satisfaction I added the rabbit to the rest and began working my way up along the hedge with the wind blowing through it towards us. This decision to leave the game cached meant that I had to change my shooting plans. Originally I had intended executing a simple half circle against the wind most of the way leaving the centre of the shoot until the afternoon. Now I planned a small complete circle which would bring me back to the game and leave a similar area for the afternoon.

Perhaps it was as well that I made that decision. It certainly seemed to work out favourably. I had barely reached the end of the hedge with Max in front of me steadily working the undergrowth before I saw him freeze into a perfect picture point, front paw crooked, tail, nose and back in a straight line. This time I knew what to expect, or thought I did. A wily old cock who had heard the shots had taken cover in the hedge.

I gave Max the signal and stood by for the expected cock rocketing from the hedgerow. Instead there was a low whirr and I caught a glimpse of a hen pheasant's grey brown plumage parallel to the ground and cunningly only a couple of feet up. A moment later she made the mistake of rising above the level of the hedge for an instant and I took a snap shot with the choke. A long-range shot and I wasn't by any means sure that I had her. It seemed to me that she faltered a moment before disappearing from sight. Confound it. Had I only wounded her for nothing? For a moment I wondered. Perhaps it was a clean miss. Still it was worth putting the dog in anyway.

"Hie Lost, Max."

Off he went like a rocket without waiting for any second bidding. He'd seen the bird above the hedge and he knew where to look. Or did he? I began to wonder as he ran down this side of the hedge for fifty yards past the place. Drat the dog! I pursed my lips to whistle him off and set him on the line but a moment later I stopped. He knew what he was about all right. He checked a moment. Then he was off again down the hedge at speed. Then he checked once more. Miraculously he had the hen, a strong runner, just tipped in the right wing, in his mouth.

As he came back towards me I marvelled inwardly. He must have followed her down the hedge accurately from the other side to the one she was on. Then she made the mistake of wriggling through a gap and she was almost into his jaws. For the hundredth time I told myself that the dog knows best. It simply never pays to interfere but many times it does seem impossible that he can be right.

I took the pheasant from him and apologised for my doubts about him. There was no doubt which of us was responsible for that addition to the bag anyway. Max, however, took my apologies and my congratulations with the same air of happy indifference. It was obvious that there was only one thing he was interested in and that was getting on with the day's shooting. With my ego suitably deflated I turned into the next field.

Now we had the wind across us as we turned to the right in a slow circle. I worked Max by hand signals closer in to avoid any game being set up out of gun shot. In this way we worked across the field when to my surprise Max made a perfect point down wind. I advanced towards him dubiously. Sometimes I had seen him point the spot which a covey had just left where the scent was still strong and I felt this must be a similar understandable mistake.

A moment later, however, there was a whirr of wings and a covey was off at my approach. I was taken by surprise and I nearly forgot to fire. As it was I made too hasty a shot with my first and I saw my bird falter slightly and fly on with one leg hanging. Fortunately I was still able to give him the other barrel and bring him down. Perhaps he would have towered and come down anyway, but I prefer to make sure even if it does mean wasting a shot. Better to repair the damage of a hasty shot than make matters worse by hesitating and possibly making another mistake.

I may just have imagined the look of disgust on Max's face as I retrieved the bird myself or I may not. He enjoys retrieving and he doesn't like it when I go off and do it myself. Nor does he like it when I miss altogether as happens only too often. But he can't, after all, have it both ways. I agreed that I had made a botch of matters through not believing in him and we continued across the field.

By this time more than an hour had passed and I was beginning to congratulate myself on the bag. Even allowing for the fact that there should have been an extra partridge, I had been doing even better than I had expected. While I was thus mentally congratulating myself, I suddenly became aware that Max was still. I must have been unconsciously eyeing him while I day-dreamed, for I was aware that he had frozen almost at the same moment as it happened. Then in an instant I was alert.

This time it turned out to be another big buck hare, which made the mistake of running right across in front of me. Possibly because I had been day-dreaming I made extra certain of him and he turned a somersault at thirty-five yards satisfyingly cleanly shot. As he was on the edge of the boundary ditch and partially concealed by long stubble I sent Max off to fetch him. Generally speaking I believe in picking up dead game lying in the open even if it means a little extra trouble, but in this instance it meant Max would have to use his nose to find it and I knew he would enjoy the work.

It is always interesting to watch how he sets about finding game like that. First he ran forward to the place he had last seen it and then his nose went down and up, and down again, and he was off, hardly pausing, in a direct line for the hare. A satisfied tail wag as he reached the hare and a careful adjustment of his jaws as he picked it up by the back. Then he returned with his tail going and a pleased look on his face as he held his head high to avoid it trailing.

These big hares can be a considerable strain on a dog, but Max has always been able to carry them at a gallop with his head up for considerable distances. Of course he is a big powerful dog and it is no great effort for him. It is obvious, however, that if the hare was still alive and kicking that it would be a different matter. Anyone who sends his dog after a live hare is asking for him to become hard-mouthed. It is almost a physical impossibility for them to pick up the hare unless they have finished him off by 'closing the suitcase'.

By the time I had this hare in the bag along with the pheasant and the partridge I felt it was time that I started to turn for my cache of game. I reckoned that it would take me probably another half hour to finish my circle and by that time I would be ready for my lunch.

While I was busy distributing the load on my back, Max had retired to the ditch for a well earned drink of water and now at my whistle he did not come. Suspecting what had happened I went forward three or four paces and found him rigidly on point once more with his head bent back half over his shoulder. At my approach a rabbit bolted from the patch of grass he was pointing and stupidly ran along the edge of the ditch. Before it could change its mind and seek cover again, I bowled it over with a snap shot.

So far I had been shooting above my form and I was congratulating myself on the fact when the inevitable happened. Half way across the next field, with Max working to one side of me and slightly in advance so that we covered the ground between us, he abruptly came on point. I advanced at the ready and as I did so he moved slowly and pointed once more. I knew what that meant. A cock pheasant in the open moving ahead of us. But this one hadn't yet learned to run ahead of the gun and dog. It was flushed almost at once.

With that characteristic 'Urc-urc-urc-urc-urc' of alarm it rocketed straight upwards into the sun. Accustomed as I am to pheasants' eccentricities I hadn't been expecting that and I put in a hurried shot which I knew, as I fired it, was a clean miss. Furious with myself I steadied up and brought him down with the second barrel, but even that wasn't a clean kill. I saw him pick himself up and set off with the determined look of a bird in a hurry to go somewhere.

However, I was equally determined not to be hurried

this time and I took my time about giving Max the command to be after him. Then at last, 'Hie Lost'.

Max was up at once with an eager expression, and off in the direction I waved. No need to set him on the exact spot the bird landed. He was quite capable of finding that for himself. Sure enough he was on to it in a moment and off like a flash. Straight for the far hedge he headed as fast as he could gallop. Now I began to wonder whether I hadn't been rash in not setting him off at once. If the cock made the hedge perhaps he would lose him. For a moment or two I was on tenterhooks as he reached the hedge and disappeared. There were momentary glimpses of liver and white as he worked up the hedge. Surely the bird wouldn't have gone that way? Now he was plunging away down in that far corner. Must be the best part of three hundred and fifty yards. Surely he'd lost him. No. Good boy! He had it.

Can there be anything more satisfying than the knowledge that your dog has carried out a really good retrieve. There was no doubt that pheasant was a strong runner. Shot in the wing and the body as he was, he still managed to travel the best part of four hundred yards. Definitely a little praise had been well earned. Good boy!

Next another field and nothing turned up. We had been shooting all round this area and came into it down wind so it was scarcely surprising that all the game had gone. Here we returned to the cache. Quite a satisfactory addition to be made to it for the morning's work. Another hare, another rabbit, one more partridge and a brace of pheasants. All very satisfactory.

After a leisurely lunch shared with Max and topped off with a cup of coffee and a pipe, it was time to start again. The circle planned for the afternoon was bigger and bordered the river at one point so there was always the chance of duck. With the morning's bag safely stowed away we started with high hopes and a certain dangerous complacency.

The first field proving a blank did something to remove the complacency. In the next field Max froze on point before I was properly over the fence. I just had time to get myself clear of the barbed wire before the covey that had been lying there were off at the sound of my approach. I managed to snap-shot with the choke and saw the outside bird I had picked topple. It looked like a runner, however, so I gave Max the signal to be after it. Rather to my surprise it turned out to be stone-dead and he picked it without any difficulty.

The rest of the field proved blank but now we arrived at the river bank. Here almost at once Max froze on point at a likely clump of reeds. Uncertain whether it was duck or pheasant I advanced cautiously. Then one of those things happened. Just to my right a hare got up. For a moment I was tempted to ignore it. Perhaps I should have done. It wasn't Max's fault because as yet he hadn't covered that piece of ground. The question was should I take it and possibly miss the chance of a crack at the game he was pointing. I took it.

The hare was crossing me from left to right and I gave it plenty of lead and had the satisfaction of seeing him bowled over. A moment later I swung round in time to see a cock pheasant streaking across the river and Max going down with a slightly surprised look on his face. I took a quick snap shot at the pheasant and saw him land with a splash in the reeds on the far side of the river. All eminently satisfactory. A warm glow of achievement spread through me and I began to congratulate myself.

As I advanced a couple of paces, a brace of mallard that had been lying below the reeds got up and flew bellies to the surface of the river like a pair of jet-propelled paddle boats. And I was still unloaded. What a fool! How I cursed myself. Just in case, but much too late, I reloaded and sent Max across the river to pick up the pheasant.

While he was busy I walked across to pick up the hare. As I did so I put up another. The fields seemed to be teeming with them. It was a long-range shot and I barely gave enough allowance for the speed he was moving at. I saw him leap high and falter and I knew I had hit him in the lung but he didn't stop. I marked carefully the point he made for in the hedge and decided to put Max on when we reached the spot.

Picking up the hare, I went back in time to find him climbing up the bank with the pheasant in his mouth. At least he had had no difficulty with that one.

Taking him slowly up the river bank I managed to pick off a couple of rabbits but we came across nothing else until we reached the spot in the hedge where the hare had gone through. Here I gave Max the command 'Hie Lost'.

He looked at me eagerly and cast around for a moment or two. Then he was off and along the hedge with an air of purpose. I was content to follow him and watch. I had a feeling it might be worth it and sure enough it was. He went off too fast for me to be sure how far he travelled, but I was in time to see him coming back through the hedge at the end of the field with the carcase of the hare in his mouth. As I thought, it had been shot through the lung as the bright-red blood round its muzzle showed. Yet all the same it must have travelled more than a quarter of a mile before dropping dead.

By the time I had stowed it inside the game bag I began to feel the time had come for home. Accordingly I had turned and was making tracks in the required direction when Max froze once more ahead of me. In order to make certain of the shot I had to ease the game bag on my shoulder. A few moments later I was picking up yet another hare. This time I was determined that enough was as good as a feast. But not so Max. When I reached the scene of my cache and deposited the fresh load with relief I turned to find Max frozen into yet another statuesque point some twenty yards upwind.

I was by this time in two minds as to whether to shoot or not. Still undecided, but attracted unwillingly by the urgency of his pose, I walked up to him and gave him the signal to flush. A final hare set off at a canter to be added to the bag before he had gone more than thirty yards. At this time hares with us were almost as much of a pest as rabbits and had to be shot. This brought the grand total to seven hares, four rabbits, a brace and a half of pheasants, and a couple of brace of partridges. On the whole I had been shooting well. Max had carried out some splendid retrieves and behaved like a Field Trial champion. It had been a good day.

TEN

A Blank Day

IN CASE anyone has received the misguided impression that shooting with a general-purpose Pointer-Retriever in some magic way ensures that there will be game to be shot at, I will try to disillusion them with an account of a blank day. It does not follow, however, that a blank day need necessarily be a boring day or even a dull or uninteresting day. There is plenty to observe and learn from the conduct of the dog and usually there is plenty of scope for improvement.

The day in question began very much as many another December shooting day. The sky was suspiciously leaden with a red ball of sun appearing dimly in a misty haze, but there was a sharpness of frost in the air and the ground was crisp. Altogether it looked as if scenting conditions would be good and game plentiful. We set out together with high hopes and started up the first hedge optimistically.

There was little doubt in my mind that we ought to find a pheasant or two in the hedgerows with the frost we had been having and Max seemed to think so too. With the wind coming straight across us I worked him on the far side of the hedge to begin with. Then it became too thick for me to see him and I whistled to him to come through, one short recall blast on my so-called silent whistle. The immediate effect was to bring Max through

the hedge with an enquiring look on his face and to set
up half a dozen pigeons which had been sitting in a tree
just ahead of us safely out of range. So much for the
silence of a silent whistle. I avoided Max's reproachful
look and tried to pretend it didn't matter. But neither of
us were fooled. As usual in such instances I felt like kicking
myself. However it's all in the luck of the game and it's
best to try to be philosophical about it.

As we followed the hedge down and turned the corner
on to the continuation of it I began to wonder. By the
time we had walked for another twenty minutes or so
without even a rabbit forthcoming I began to wonder
even more. Then there was a twang of wire ahead of us
as a heavy body squeezed through the fence. I jumped
towards the hedge and craned my neck over just in time
to see a russet-red form slip along the furrow of the
ploughed field on the other side. So that was the answer.
We had been following in the tracks of a fox. I should
have realised earlier.

For a moment I meditated letting blast a barrel, for we
are a non-hunting county and foxes have to be shot, but
he was too far away. There is never any point in shooting
at anything when it is out of range. In this connection it
always seems to me that the average shot has no real idea
of distance, or what his shot patterns look like at different
ranges, otherwise some of the shots I have seen attempted
would never have been fired. From this point of view it
is well worth while watching your dog in front of you and
mentally checking his distance from you. By pacing a
range in a handy paddock and fixing in the mind's eye
the distances with the dog present it is surprisingly easy
to accustom oneself to judging distance automatically.
In order to shoot effectively with or without a dog it
might almost be said to be a necessity to do so.

In this particular instance I knew the fox was out of

range and left it at that. Had I fired it is possible that the
cartridges might have balled or some fluky pellets might
have penetrated a vital spot. Even then, however, he
would not have been stopped. He would have gone off
to die an unpleasant lingering death of gangrene. In all
probability it would simply have been a complete waste of
cartridges as well as alarming the game in the vicinity
unnecessarily.

As we went on, however, I began to wonder whether
there was any game to be alarmed. Max patiently continued to work the ditch and hedge, but nothing moved,
and he very seldom showed any signs of interest to indicate
that something had at least passed that way. Altogether
it looked like being a dud morning, for by this time an
hour or more had passed and we had covered a lot of
ground without sighting any game. Then I heard the
sound.

"Oink, oink."

I looked up quickly and I saw them coming towards me
in the distance. Geese. A skein in line ahead. Sweeping
towards me in beautifully exact formation. In a moment
I was in the ditch with Max, taking cover behind what
undergrowth was left. I knew there was just a chance
they might come down, for the field was stubble undersown
with clover, which was peeping through and very tempting
feed for geese. Also I knew from past experience that they
often did come down in these particular fields where I was
lying when the weather was hard. So I lay trying to look
as much like a bush as I could manage and held my breath
as they came on.

"Oink, oink, oink, oink."

They began to circle round now. There must have been
about thirty of them. It seemed like hundreds. The noise
they made talking to each other was wonderful, but they
weren't going to be caught easily. They swept down

towards me. Closer, closer. Did I dare to shoot yet? No.
They were about double the range still. Were they really?
No? Yes? Drat! They'd seen us. A moment later they
were climbing again, circling round higher and higher.

Max looked up at me with a grin. He knew we'd only
shot two on the shoot in the last five years. He knew we
hadn't any heavy shot with us and he knew it was a
hopeless proposition shooting at them with fives unless
they were well within range. However, I believe he really
enjoys seeing geese come down and the noise they make,
almost as much as I do. Often when they've come over
in the winter time I've noticed him cock his head and
look at me with a query in his eyes.

Never mind. We continued on our way cheered at the
first sign of the geese on the shoot that year. Perhaps
we'd get them later on. Meanwhile it looked as if it
would be worth while trying the fields we were on for a
hare or a covey of partridges. We turned and started to
cross the nearest stubble field. At a wave from me, Max
started quartering to windward, occasionally casting an
eye towards me to keep his position correctly, as I wanted
it.

The weather had begun to change now, however.
There was a hint of snow in the air and still we seemed to
be unlucky. A hare moved a long way ahead of us dis-
turbed by the sound of our approach. It was interesting
to watch Max come across the spot and check for an
instant some paces away before his nose told him what
had happened and that the hare's form was vacant.
Then we reached the edge of another field and I saw him
pause just in advance and stiffen, head up.

Arriving at the hedge, I saw at once what had attracted
his attention. About fifty yards away there was a roe deer
standing like a statue looking at us. It was the first of its
species I had seen on my shoot though I knew there were

many close at hand. Even as I looked, it was off with a startled bound and then in a graceful leap up and over the fence at the boundary. For a moment I watched fascinated. There was no chance of a shot of course and anyway I hated the thought of trying to shoot one with a twelve-bore, even if it had been in range. I know they can do a lot of damage but there really aren't enough of them in this part of the world to worry about.

Max, I was interested to notice, seemed almost as fascinated as I was. I went forward with him to the spot where the deer had been standing and I was interested to see how deeply instinct was ingrained in him for he stiffened at the scent again, although I am almost certain that he had never seen one before.

However, the weather had begun to look threatening and the sky was turning rapidly even more leaden so we did not linger there. I moved on with Max into the field of roots which, no doubt, had attracted the roe deer originally. Here I kept Max ranging close in within gunshot, although the turnips were sparse enough on the ground to let him go further, and inside a few minutes he had frozen on his first point of the day.

Advancing up on him cautiously I saw that he was holding a plump, well-fed hen pheasant under cover of a couple of roots. As I wasn't shooting hens I took it as a good opportunity to make him come to heel with a signal, hand smartly tapped against thigh. There is no doubt it pays to vary one's orders occasionally to make certain that the dog obeys every command. I could see his look of pained astonishment and his eyebrows went up but he made no other signs. Again I tapped my thigh firmly and this time I gave a low recall whistle as well. This time, reluctantly, he obeyed me and came to heel. At that moment, of course, the pheasant chose to scuttle off audibly rustling the turnips and for a second he was

tempted to turn. A stern 'No' checked him and he took
up his station at heel with a suitably ashamed expression.
I kept him there for a moment or two and then sent him
off on range again.

The roots seemed full of the life that the hedgerows had
been lacking that day and in a few moments he was
pointing once more. As it was rather suspiciously close to
where I thought the hen pheasant had gone I advanced
rather carelessly. I was in an awkward patch of rutted
ground when the cock pheasant I had not been expecting
rocketed out with tail feathers trailing. In trying to get
my foothold I trod on a root and nearly went down. By
the time I had sorted myself out that particular cock was
well out of harm's way. I did my best to avoid meeting
Max's accusing gaze.

We went on towards the end of the roots in silence,
with Max adopting a pose of injured dignity and
efficiency which I found particularly irritating. After all,
as I pointed out, anyone can slip on roots occasionally.
Apart from that, I added, we didn't really want to shoot
every cock. After all, unless a balanced number of
pheasants were shot, there wouldn't be any mates for the
hens that were preserved. But argument and excuses
were of no avail. I have yet to meet anything that
matches Max's look of scorn when I have missed a shot,
after he has found, pointed and flushed the game, as all
too frequently happens.

However, sometimes the tables are reversed and for
once I was to have the pleasure of seeing it happen. A few
moments later, leaving the field of roots, we crossed over a
small stream by a wooden sleeper bridge. As Max leaped
over it just ahead of me there was a sudden awe-inspiring
swish of wings. A split second later something large and
attenuated with a snake-like neck and yellow beak and
legs shot past his nose. The wide wing span for a brief

hare is pointed . . .

shed and shot.

Retrieved.

instant made me think of goose, then of course I recognised it. A heron. Again a stranger to these parts. The first I had seen on my shoot.

I watched it fly off rapidly at first and then more slowly with deceptively lazy beats of its great wing span. Then my attention was brought back to the stream as Max fell in with a loud splash. Startled by the heron, he had lost his balance and fallen in. As he scrambled out looking shamefaced and foolish I felt I had had my revenge. However, the weather was not going to allow us to continue.

As I turned with him the first snow flakes began to fall, and soon they were coming thicker and thicker. The landscape was gradually blotted out by a curtain of swirling whiteness. Visibility was nil. There was nothing left to do but turn for home. The mystery of why no game had been moving was explained. In common with most animals, if they sense an approaching blizzard, they tuck themselves in and prepare to stick it out in comfort. I decided the best thing I could do was to follow their example.

Walking up the hedge in shelter from the driving blast of the snow I saw some birds flying ahead of me. For a moment I paused before I recognised them as lapwings, better known as peewits, a form of plover. Although common enough in some places, they are again rarities on my shoot. Apart from the fact that lapwings are protected, I don't believe in shooting any plover. They are a useful bird, not very good eating, and when shot are merely a pathetic bundle of feathers. So in due course I returned home with an empty game bag and without the gun being fired.

Yet even though it was a blank day and even though the gun had to be cleaned and dried, notwithstanding when I returned I still felt it had been worth it. I had seen a fox,

I

and geese at close quarters. I had seen a roe deer and a heron, none of which I had seen on my shoot before. I had seen Max working in unusual circumstances and I had been able to teach him that even when he had pointed it didn't necessarily mean that I was going to ask him to flush. That in itself was a lesson which was well timed for he had lately been getting into the habit of assuming too easily that I wanted him to flush the game and almost jumping the signal.

It would, it is true, have been more agreeable if I had brought back a cock pheasant for the larder but it and the hen would live to breed another day, I reflected. That is if the fox didn't manage to get them before I did. However, Max and I would do our best to see that didn't happen if we could help it. Even out of the shooting season there is still plenty to do with a dog like him. Vermin to be kept down and nests and young coveys to be protected.

Decidedly one blank day now and then does no one any harm and every sportsman must expect it. Nor does it follow that because a day was blank it was any the less enjoyable. When one looks back at them in retrospect one sees that it is often the day when least was shot which proves the more memorable, for all the lack of the bag.

ELEVEN

A Day's Partridge Shooting

I MAKE no excuse for including an account of a day's
partridge shooting at driven birds in a book on
roughshooting. It has been emphasised frequently that
it is always advisable to give the general-purpose dog as
much variety as possible. Should the roughshooter be
fortunate enough to receive any invitations to attend such
a shoot, he should accept them if possible. The fact that he
is advancing his dog's education as well as enjoying a
change of sport himself should merely serve to increase his
pleasure in the day. I am lucky enough to have friends in
East Anglia in ideal partridge country and this is a
description of a day there which I can still remember
clearly.

By half-past nine the usual group of small boys in oil-
skins who were to act as beaters had assembled on the
lawn in front of the house. Near them was the smaller
group of adults led by Alec, the head keeper. Around
them, mainly on leash, were a motley selection of
labradors, springers and spaniels. Soon, as the guns began
to arrive, the number of dogs and people on the lawn
increased. About this time a short dialogue ensued between
our host and Alec.

"We'll start with the Mill Field from the top end then,
Alec?"

"Arr. Beater's 're all here. There'll be a tidy few

coveys in they roots. Reckon us'll hev a wet marnin' uv it. Better be off wi' them naow."

"Right, Alec. We're moving on to the Main Road then, aren't we?"

"Thass right, sir. Should be a good few pheasants in the cover up there tew."

With that Alec collected his beaters and started off up the drive. Meanwhile the guns moved in closer and introductions were made, where necessary, and the conversation moved on to dogs and guns and the prospect of the day's sport. Then the draw took place. I found myself number three next to George, a jovial Norfolk farmer and old friend, on one side, and a Brigadier whom I had never met before on the other side. George was temporarily without a dog, but the Brigadier had a large liver and white Springer which looked as if it might have made a useful general-purpose dog although it was straining at its leash and panting to be off. There were seven guns in all and four dogs, including Max, and we made a cavalcade of some four cars as we started off to the Mill Field.

As we were beginning to sort ourselves out in the gateway of the field, Max froze into a perfect picture point, head, back and tail in a straight line and foreleg raised, a few yards along the hedge.

"There's a pheasant in the hedge," I said firmly, but not without inward misgivings, to my host. "Do you want it shot or not?"

"Oh? We've got to cross this field anyway," he replied cheerfully. "Let's see how your dog works. Shoot it by all means. We're shooting hens today."

I gave Max the signal and fortunately he flushed a fine cock pheasant from the hedgerow. It rocketed upwards with a characteristic 'Urc, urc, urc'. As Max went down automatically, I allowed the bird sufficient law and then fired. The cock's wings folded satisfactorily and he plummeted earthwards the other side of the hedge.

After a moment's pause I signalled Max on with a 'Hie Lost' and a few moments later he was wriggling back through the hedge with the bird in his mouth, then sitting in front of me to deliver it to hand. It was a good augury of the day to come and I decided that even if he did not distinguish himself again, he had at least started off well.

Not many minutes later we were taking our places in front of the old mill from which the field took its name. The Brigadier I noticed was having a little trouble with his Springer which was tugging wildly at its leash. I sympathised with him, but at the same time, in case his example was liable to be demoralising, I slipped Max on to the lead also. He looked up at me rather indignantly with his brow furrowing in the very expressive way he has, but I refused to take any notice.

A few moments later the sound of a distant whistle brought everyone's attention to their front. Seconds later a fusillade of shots on our right indicated that a covey had swept over at the other end of the line. Placed as we were, we could not see how the shooting had gone. From the number of shots, and knowing the company, I decided it had probably been a good start to the day. I noticed Max's ears cocked and the Springer bounding forward almost towing the Brigadier with it in its eagerness.

Another warning whistle alerted us and a moment later it was our turn. A covey flying low and fast came swooping over the hedge top at full speed between the Brigadier and myself. I just managed to drop one in front and then swung round to take another with my second barrel behind. The second, I was displeased to note, looked like a runner.

After that it was fast and furious, with George on my

left taking a beautiful left and right in front of him as I
reloaded. I remember getting three more birds, one in
front and two behind, and the rest of the line were more or
less the same. Then the beaters appeared and the work of
picking the birds started. My own I was able to collect
fairly quickly except for the first runner. I sent Max off
after this and I was pleased to see he had obviously
marked it for he went straight to the spot where it had
dropped and after a swift cast round his head went down
and he was off.

"He can certainly move," commented George, beside
me in approving tones. "Is he on that first one of
yours?"

"I hope so, anyway," I grinned.

As I spoke Max halted and cast round once more. A
moment later he was off again, then he checked abruptly
and miraculously the partridge was in his mouth. Less
than a minute later he was sitting in front of me with the
live bird in his jaws.

"Not bad at all," applauded George, which was high
praise for him. "Can he do that on pheasant too?"

"Given the opportunity he can," I replied confidently.

"I say there," bellowed the Brigadier at that moment.
"Do you mind bringing that dog of yours over here? I
daren't let this wild young devil loose, I'm afraid. There's
a right and left stone dead over here somewhere."

I came forward willingly enough and set Max off on the
spot indicated with a wave and 'Hie Lost'. He circled
round quickly with an air of purpose, but the first circle
produced no visible reaction. He cast round a second
time wider, of his own accord, and this time, at the
perimeter of the circle, he hit a scent and his head went
down and he was off at speed.

"He's gone wild, too, hasn't he?" asked the Brigadier
tactlessly.

"No, he hasn't," I retorted loyally. "It's just that your right and left must have been strong runners."

Privately I wondered if the Brigadier hadn't been rather optimistic. By this time Max had vanished into a ditch at the bottom of the field and I was wondering whether to call him off. A moment later I was relieved to see him reappear, with something in his jaws. On delivery it turned out to be a strong runner very much alive. Apart from the tip of one wing it seemed quite unhurt. I handed it to the Brigadier.

"Your bird?" I asked.

"Mm. Ha. Yes. Perhaps they were both runners," he returned brazenly. "Difficult to tell sometimes isn't it? Better not waste any more time trying to find the other, though. Thanks all the same."

George and I exchanged amused smiles as we walked back to the cars again. The next stand was at the so-called Main Road and to get there we had to return to the cars and then walk across a stretch of disused aerodrome which was still full of patches of tangled brambles and barbed wire. At one of the many overgrown tangles of undergrowth Max froze into another point, forepaw raised and head lowered.

"Looks like another pheasant," I said turning to George. "Will you take it or shall I?"

"You go ahead," he answered.

I gave Max the signal to flush and a moment later a cock pheasant was streaking away at ground level with an explosion of 'Urc-urc-urc'. I took the shot rather carelessly and did not allow for the fact that it was flying away at an angle. It came down but it looked a strong and determined runner disappearing across the concrete runway into the undergrowth on the other side.

"Hie Lost, Max," I ordered.

He was off in a flash, but even as he moved two more cocks and a couple of hens, which had all been in the neighbourhood, rose together. For a moment the air seemed full of excited pheasants and I was in the middle of reloading. George took a calm left and right as I slammed my gun shut and fired simultaneously with the Brigadier behind me.

"My bird, I think," said the Brigadier coolly as the bird I had aimed at fell dead. "Pity your dog flushed them all at once like that."

I glared at him furiously, bereft of speech by his calm audacity. Fortunately Max returned at that moment with the cock he had been sent for, studiously ignoring the birds flapping on the concrete runway he was crossing. By the time I had accepted the bird from him I had recovered myself. After all it might have been the Brigadier's bird quite genuinely, though I was still reasonably sure it wasn't. In any case it wasn't worth making a fuss about.

We picked up the birds on the runway and walked on at speed to catch up with the others. I noticed with a certain amount of satisfaction that the Brigadier's Springer was straining at the leash even more strongly. It was obvious from the way they were both panting that neither of them got enough exercise. However, we were only just in time to reach our stands before the whistle was being blown and the birds were coming over again.

As Alec had suggested, there was a higher percentage of pheasants on this drive and they were coming over with the wind behind them at speed. The partridges too seemed to have been split up more for they were coming singly or in pairs rather than in coveys. This always makes for more exciting shooting and the next twenty minutes or so passed very quickly. I remember one high bird which towered well out behind me and a startling shot of the

Brigadier's which brought down a pair in front of him, both strong runners by the look of them.

At the end of the drive George called over to me as we were collecting our birds.

"Bring your dog over here. There's a runner gone back into the hedge," he cried.

"Hold on a moment," I replied.

I sent Max off first after the bird that had towered. A wave and the order 'Hie Lost' were all that was required. He had marked it well. I watched with satisfaction as he went steadily out into the field and finally cast round to pick up the scent and almost at once was on to the dead bird. Having brought that to hand I set him into the hedge for George's runner.

"I don't think it'll have gone far," said George confidently.

Contrary to his expectations, however, Max started moving down the hedge at speed after a slight check to begin with. After wriggling through what seemed an impossibly small gap, he came back with a strong runner. As soon as I had taken it, however, he was off again and almost at once returned with a dead bird which had been lying partially concealed in the hedge.

"That's the Brigadier's bird he got," I exclaimed as the answer dawned on me. "He must have been on to yours and the scent of the other crossed it, so he brought them both."

The reason for his slight check at the start was more than amply explained. As we moved on to the next stand I was feeling very pleased with him and George was still commenting on a fine piece of work. This time, however, I was on the end of the line at number seven for the last beat of the morning and nothing much broke my way. Apart from one old hen pheasant that tried to fly out past a thicket, I shot nothing. When it came to retrieving,

however, it turned out that Max had to work hard, for the
bird had landed in the heart of the bramble grown
thicket and even to force an entry was a job in itself.
However, he returned with the bird showing a few signs
of its rough passage but otherwise unharmed. After that
we adjourned for a picnic lunch. A welcome sandwich and
a glass of beer and a chat.

After lunch, feeling somewhat replete and satisfied with
ourselves, we returned to the fray. Fortunately for most of
us the birds in the afternoon showed some signs of being
slower than the birds in the morning. Perhaps we were
swinging faster and our reactions were quicker or perhaps
the birds were tiring. Whatever the reason, they seemed
to me to be easier to hit. This usually seems to me to be
the case. However I noticed that for my neighbour the
Brigadier it was apparently not so. Like Mr. Pickwick he
showed signs of wanting to find a convenient place in the
shade, but there were no wheelbarrows handy.

At the first stand of the afternoon he remained in a
trance as the birds streamed over him. Then to add insult
to injury he woke up in time to fire both barrels at what
was clearly my bird and miss it. Fortunately our host,
who was two places up the line, saw what was going on
and he was not a man to suffer that sort of thing in
silence, especially having been in the Navy himself.

"Wake up you ruddy Pongo, and stop poaching," he
bellowed caustically down the line.

There was a chorus of appreciative laughter from the
beaters who had approached close enough, and a number
of sotto voce comments which caused the Brigadier to
turn a deep magenta colour. However he turned out to
be not such a bad fellow after all for while we were
picking up the birds he came over and apologised.

" 'Fraid that was your bird," he said. "Sorry about it.
More than half asleep on my feet. Deserved that rocket."

"That's all right," I assured him.

"Like the way that dog of yours shapes," he went on. "He's done some smart work today."

I began to feel a genuine warmth towards him. He wasn't nearly as bad as I had thought at first. At least he had the tact to make up for a bad start by praising Max.

There was no time for more before we changed stands, but at least the atmosphere had thawed perceptibly and thereafter the afternoon was pure pleasure. George was shooting excellently and suddenly the Brigadier picked up surprisingly, too. There is something about a good example out shooting that helps. Anyway, I know I felt inspired also and nothing seemed to go wrong. I picked off two rights and lefts in front in succession and I had one high bird that was swerving down the front of the line which will long remain in my memory. Max sat quietly marking his birds and carried out his retrieves without mistakes.

So the afternoon passed until the light began to fail and the last stand of all was reached. This backed on to an old marl pit surrounded by trees and filled with water, as is usually the way. One of the runners Max retrieved for me after it was over, took him to the edge of this pit and, as soon as he had brought it to hand, he returned at once to the edge of the pit and froze on point.

"Come on, George," I suggested. "Let's see what it is."

George, who by this time had developed a healthy respect for Max's points, joined me willingly. As we approached the edge of the pit together we were both prepared for a cock pheasant, but, before I could give Max the signal to flush, a brace of mallard took off in front of us. Both of us fired at once and afterwards we each claimed that we fired at the same one in turn. Whoever was responsible, both birds fell with a splash into the pit. In a moment, at the command 'Hie Lost', Max was in after them. A few minutes later we rejoined the party with two fat ducks and one wet dog, all thoroughly pleased with ourselves.

There remained but the pleasant tasks of counting the bag, drying off the dog and gathering round the fire with a drink to discuss the day's shooting and to talk of dogs and guns until it was once more time to return home. Another day's sport was over.

TWELVE

A Day's Pheasant Shooting

I CAN never make up my mind whether I prefer driven partridges or driven pheasant. When I am shooting at one I am sure I prefer it to the other, but as soon as I change over to the other the reverse holds good. At times I feel there is nothing more difficult to shoot than those deceptively high pheasants hurtling over the treetops, and at other times that there is more skill required for a successful right and left in front out of a covey of driven partridges coming straight over the top of a hedge and exploding in all directions. I usually end up by going out by myself with the dog and missing several walked up 'sitters' and returning suitably chastened, or else firmly reminding myself that wildfowling is really far more sport than either of them.

The fact is that nothing in shooting is a certainty since the margin of human error is too great to make it otherwise. A considerable degree of the pleasure in shooting is derived from the satisfaction of overcoming that uncertainty. If economists and psychologists and all the other '-ists' who base their researches on the human mind and body would remember that no individual can be expected to produce the same reactions in the same situation every time, especially with another uncertain quantity such as an animal involved, they would accept that any pretence at scientific exactness in measuring those reactions is out of the question.

As far as my shooting is concerned I am only too aware that my high pheasant shooting leaves much to be desired. I am fortunate, however, in living fairly close to what has justly been described as one of the best high pheasant shoots in Scotland, to which I am occasionally invited. The main part of the shoot is along a narrow glen with steep wooded sides. The guns stand down below and the slopes are beaten so that the birds fly out over the glen with the result that very often the stranger to the shoot does not even bother to raise his gun, considering the birds out of range. The practised shot however will soon disillusion him. Then there is plenty of work for a dog, crossing the burn, which runs along the foot of the glen, and searching for dead birds and runners on the wooded slopes.

The particular shoot I have in mind was a New Year's Day shoot three years ago. There were only six guns out and, as the retrieving is usually done by the keeper's dogs, Max was the only dog in the line. My neighbours on either side were Henry and David, both old hands at these high pheasants, with the knack, for knack it undoubtedly is, of bringing them down. It was a pleasant, tingling morning and everyone was in good spirits. I knew that, even if I was not on form, as I seldom am at these birds, Max would have plenty of work to do.

We started off by moving to our places at the end of a long narrow plantation, with the beaters advancing towards us. Here I was one of the outlying guns and to begin with little broke my way. As I was standing tensed and waiting with Max sitting at my heels, ears cocked and ready, I suddenly spotted a stealthy movement in the trees. As a cock pheasant sped down the far side of the trees and a perfect single shot far to my right crumpled him into a ball of feathers in mid air, I saw an unmistakable head with pricked ears appear at the fence.

A fox. We live in a non-hunting county and foxes are shot on sight so I did not hesitate. In order to be quite sure I gave him both barrels for good measure. One quick backward jump in the air and he disappeared from sight.

Of course it followed inevitably that before I had time to reload the only pheasant of that stand flew out over me like an express. However, it was only a few moments later that the beaters appeared and I sent Max off to retrieve the fox with a 'Hie Lost'. As I had anticipated he had no difficulty. It was lying stone dead a yard or two back from the fence. In a moment he was back carrying it proudly towards me. A fine old dog fox, grey around the muzzle.

"Good work, sir," cried my friend, the head-keeper. "I've been after yon blighter a good while now."

My chagrin over the pheasant was forgotten. To the keepers I had scored the best shot of the morning. There would be plenty more pheasants later. With this philosophical thought I turned towards the next stand. Once again I was on the outside on the top of the glen above the steep slope, walking just ahead of the beaters, acting as stop for any pheasants that might be wily enough to turn back from the guns in front below. The shots were not usually so spectacular as those from below but they could be interesting. For Max it was an enjoyable pastime as he was able to roam freely on the slope pushing out the birds with the beaters. In this he excelled, being able to reach places that the beaters were unable to attempt.

We had barely advanced more than twenty yards before the first pheasant, an old wily cock, came rocketing backwards over the treetops. I swung firmly through him and fired and had the satisfaction of seeing him crumple over the heads of the beaters, to the accompaniment of muted cheers. Before I had brought my gun down to reload, another pheasant, a hen this time, flew out of the trees in front, away from me into the sun. I swung back quickly and fired again. I saw her drop and start running back for the shelter of the trees. Poor shooting, even it if was into the sun. However, a right and left of a sort.

I passed the warning to the beaters that there was a runner ahead of them and whistled for Max. When he appeared I put him on to the line and had the satisfaction of hearing a beater cry a few moments later, "He's got your runner, sir. He's coming back to you now."

The excitement in the man's voice was evident and I wished I was more in a position to watch Max working. But one can't have everything and a series of birds flying back kept me busy for the next few minutes. I remember Max appearing with one bird as another crumpled earthwards beside him, of which he took no notice at all. Another highlight was a race across the stubble at full speed after a strong cock runner. The cock was never in sight but there must have been a red-hot scent and perfect scenting conditions for Max was after him at full speed with his head well up and he caught him after a couple of hundred yards just on the far hedge. I was so busy watching him out of the corner of my eye that I nearly missed another cock that rocketed upwards through the trees. He made too much noise, however, and I caught him at the top just as he hovered for a second prior to changing direction.

Finally we reached the curve in the glen where the drive stopped. The beaters then moved backwards and the guns took up positions on the opposite side of the glen to repeat the performance. This time I was one of the guns on the floor of the glen and Max had nothing to do except sit at heel and mark the birds. Up till now most of my birds had been easy ones and I had probably had the largest share of the bag. Now, however, I was faced with the really high birds which almost always defeat me.

If I take a right and left at them, my year's shooting is made.

To begin with I had my eye thoroughly wiped by my neighbours on either side. Then a high cock came over, tail feathers streaming out, wind behind him and moving at a deceptive speed. The two guns in front of me each let him have both barrels with no effect, then it was my turn. I swung at him and through him and gave him the choke. Rather to my surprise he folded up most satisfactorily and plunged down in a breathtaking dive earthwards to land with a heavy thump some fifty yards down the glen. That was the sort of shot that made up for all the mistakes and misses of the rest of the day. I found it hard to restrain a certain Cheshire Cat grin of complacency from stealing over my face.

However, with the birds coming over there was little time for contemplation. Clean misses on my next four shots, while my neighbours took their revenge soon removed all traces of satisfaction. Fortunately I was able to redeem myself with a last shot at a woodcock that flipped between the trees in front of me for a moment too long. Then the beaters appeared and the drive was over once more. There remained only the business of collecting the birds.

Max, I was pleased to find, had noted and marked the woodcock and responded at once to my 'Hie Lost' and wave. In a few moments he was back with it neatly held in his jaws. After that he turned in the other direction and without any prompting returned with the cock. Meanwhile the keeper's dogs were busy retrieving the birds on the hillside.

"Try sending Max in there," suggested David, as I was about to turn away. "I'm sure there's a runner in there and they don't seem to be making much headway on him."

He pointed to the tree-covered slope where there were a

K

couple of dogs visible working the cover. Accordingly I sent Max across the burn with a wave and the command 'Hie Lost'. He sprang forward eagerly and splashed through the burn in a couple of leaps. A few moments later he could be seen quartering eagerly amongst the trees.

"He's on to something," I said as I saw his head go down.

A moment later, sure enough, he started moving at speed up the slope until he came to a halt in front of a fallen tree and tried to burrow inside.

"He's after a rabbit," laughed David.

"I'll wager he isn't," I replied loyally, though with a certain inevitable inner doubt. "He knows what he's after all right."

A few moments later one of the beaters arrived on the spot.

"It's a cock all right," he reported. "Right down in the roots."

I felt rather ashamed of myself for ever having had any doubts on the matter, and I called Max back and congratulated him. Then it was time for a New Year's Day lunch in the house with appropriate libations and toasts. By the time that was over most of us were in a state of post-prandial benevolence. It is usually my rule never to eat or drink very much when shooting, but this is one of the days which have to be an exception. When we finally moved out to do battle once more there was a noticeable sluggishness about our movements, with the exception of Max, who clearly wondered why on earth we had been so long.

The first stand revealed that the standard of shooting in most cases had sadly deteriorated. David next to me was shooting, as he described it himself, 'Like a sweety wife'. Henry on the other side was not much better. I cannot say that at first I had any indication that I was going to find matters any different from them. I missed three times ingloriously in succession, simple crossing shots within easy range. Then on the second and last stand of the day suddenly I picked up.

A large cock pheasant came screaming over the trees as if jet-propelled. I had a glimpse of him through a gap and I had a moment to prepare. Almost lazily I brought the gun up and somehow I was filled with complete confidence as if foreknowledge had come upon me. I swung and fired in the same instant and the bird crumpled overhead and plunged down amongst the trees on the opposite side of the glen. Before I was really aware of it I saw another following it closely and I repeated the performance almost identically. My year's shooting was made. A right and left on the high birds.

Perhaps that was what broke the rot that had set in. Anyway, David and Henry both started to pull themselves together and after that it was a question of loading and firing as fast as the birds came over, with birds crashing earthwards most satisfyingly all round and no time to spare for anything else. I remember noticing Max's ears cocked excitedly beside me as his head turned from side to side and he noted each shot and marked the pheasants as they came down. All in all it was amongst the most satisfying half-hour's shooting I can ever remember.

Finally the beaters came in sight and the retrieving started. Max was soon across the burn and up searching the slopes above us. Ten birds he brought to me and thirty five were down at that stand alone. After that the after-noon should have been pure anti-climax, but David and Henry and I had agreed to go on to shoot duck flighting into a pond near-by and we hurried on leaving the others behind to count the bag and celebrate.

We arrived at the pond just as dusk was beginning to

fall and took up our positions as unobtrusively as possible. I was at the far end of the pool, David in the middle and Henry where the duck were likely to come in first. All depended on Henry not firing too soon. However, he had had plenty of experience at this sort of game and he could be relied on. Max and the sensible little Springer belonging to the head-keeper were the only dogs, but we knew that we could rely on them.

Soon, as it became darker, we hear the whistle of wings and the first flight of mallard circled overhead. In the shadow of our hedge we all held our breath and Max's ears cocked at the sound beside me. Twice they circled as if suspecting something, then, apparently deciding that all was safe, they came in from Henry's end. A moment later both he and David fired and there were twin splashes from the pond as two ducks at least fell. At the same instant the remaining bird flew past me and I fired also. With satisfaction I saw it veer sideways and land with a heavy thud on the slopes opposite, but it was a drake that fell with its white belly uppermost. It would not do to leave it lying in full view in the open to put off those that followed.

"Hie Lost," I said quietly to Max.

He was off like a flash and I heard him splashing through the reeds. A few moments later I could see him returning with the duck in his jaws. But before he had returned another flight of mallard appeared.

"Sit," I hissed towards him.

I believe he had already anticipated the command however, for he was down before I could repeat it. In the reeds there was little chance of him being seen and sure enough a moment later these duck, too, came circling in after the rotten potatoes on which they had been feasting the past few nights. Once more our guns spoke in turn and this time four ducks fell.

A moment or two later Max was at my side and the mallard drake was delivered safely to hand. 'Good boy'. He had withstood much temptation for, dropped as he was, with the bird in his mouth and other ducks flapping in the reeds about him, it must have been very tantalising.

After that the fun was fast and furious as the darkness fell gradually until only the black shapes of the duck against the lighter horizon in front of us were left to fire at. Still they seemed to come in with an insatiable appetite for the rotten potatoes which had been laid for them. Finally it became too dark even for the best of us. Then came the job of setting the dogs off to collect the fallen birds and the runners.

Max and the little Springer went about their job eagerly. Behind us ran the ditch down which the wounded duck automatically tried to sneak away to the river and eventually the sea. In front of us were the pond and the reeds and the hill. They quartered the ground fast together and separately, halting now and then to retrieve another duck to their respective masters. Finally we decided we must have reached the limit and we counted the bag. Twenty-two head of duck in all. Not bad for three-quarters of an hour after a full day.

As we climbed into the van to get back to the lodge and a warm fire and a drink, I felt the soaking coat of the long haired Springer and Max's damp but rapidly drying coat, and I decided once again that, other things being equal, I preferred a short-haired dog for water work any day. Although it was beginning to freeze and ice was already forming on the puddles, Max was merely industriously licking himself dry. There was no such respite for the long-haired dog however. It was going to need a thorough drying and cleaning before it was fit to be kennelled.

So yet another long day's shooting was over with a
multitude of tasks performed and Max had finished
almost as fresh as when he started. Given a good night's
rest I knew he would be fit to start the same thing over
again the following day, which was a good deal more than
could be said for his owner. However, it had been a good
day and I was aware, as were the animals, of a pleasant
feeling of contentment at the end of it.

THIRTEEN

Wildfowling

THE WILDFOWLER and the roughshooter have much in common. The individual wildfowler or roughshooter often prefers going out with just his dog or at most one companion. By the very nature of the sport itself, wildfowling, even more than roughshooting, is not suitable for large parties, but most roughshooters will be familiar with one or other of its many aspects. Though it may be only a question of waiting for the ducks to flight into a barley field, it is a form of shooting all on its own. The quarry, the size of shot, the amount of allowance to be made in the angle of shooting, as well, usually, as the scenery itself; all are different. To acquit himself well the roughshooter must be ready for all weathers and his dog must be prepared to face water without a second's hesitation.

Since I have over a mile of river on one boundary of my shoot I no longer go out on foreshore and salting as much as before. It is probably true, as a friend said, that I have grown soft and idle. It is very tempting to sit by the river at a chosen spot and wait for the duck to flight, or occasionally to make a stalking foray during the day. In dirty weather there can be as much hardship in this as any foreshore or salting can offer and, since the ducks have probably been driven inland, there is very often a good deal more sport. There is certainly always the pleasing thought that comfort is closer at hand if and when it is required. I have always subscribed to the old soldier's theory that any damned fool can be uncomfortable, but that only a thrice-damned fool makes himself more uncomfortable than he need. Admittedly, however, there are times when a nagging doubt creeps into my mind and usually then I end up on another expedition to the foreshore.

For anyone who has experienced a dawn attack or the stand to arms at dusk and dawn, there is something familiar about wildfowling on the foreshore or salting. That anxious scanning of sky and horizon in the half-light with the dusk merging into the deeper darkness of night, or the greyness slowly becoming another day; that straining of the eyes and ears and every sense to gain forewarning of movement; that momentary uncertainty as shapes seem to waver and change before you into fleeting phantoms; it is all there once more. The discomfort, the wetness and the cold, as well as the sleepiness and weariness; that may all be there also. There is only one major and very satisfactory difference. No one on this occasion should be shooting at you.

It is untrue to say that all the dawns and all the darkenings of memory merge into one glorious sunrise and sunset. Nor is it true to say they all become one dark grey streak, but it is true that when you have seen a certain number they begin to fade slightly. At least mine do. It is difficult to retain in the mind's eye each separate and distinct vivid shade of colour when they are themselves changing rapidly like a kaleidoscope of Nature, or when each is as delicate and subtly different from the next as the blended colours of the rainbow. For this reason as much as any, I find my memories of my expeditions to foreshore and saltings all seem to retain a similar background and only the events themselves seem to differ.

The poet may talk about the first blush of dawn, but the cold fact of the matter is that the first break in the sky, that first false presage of the dawn itself, a mere lightening before an even more intense darkness falls, is to most people one of the worst moments of the night. That is the hour of the mind's lowest ebb, the hour for the dawn attack, the darkest, blackest hour before the dawn itself. That is the hour when the wildfowler must take up his position, still half-asleep, feeling the cold in spite of his warmest clothes, his fingers probably freezing on his gun in spite of mittens, worst of all, possibly one or both waders full of icy water. That is the moment when you wonder whether it is in fact worth it and whether it would not have been far more sensible to lie in bed. In extreme cases you may begin to doubt the sanity of anyone who commits such deliberate masochism of the flesh.

There are two things that can sustain you remarkably well in such circumstances and I am excluding the welcome nip from a hip flask or the steaming thermos of coffee and rum. The two never-failing revivers of the spirit at its darkest hour are the consciousness of a faithful companion at your heels and the sound of the wildfowl calling. The knowledge that the wildfowl are there and that you have a companion, albeit a four-legged one, is always likely to stiffen the weakening spirit.

It is, of course, not always possible to hear the geese or the duck calling to each other. It may be blowing half a gale and you may not be able to hear a thing. But when I can hear them I always experience a similar feeling of pleasure. There are few sounds better to my mind than that of wildfowl talking to each other. Perhaps the only other sound to equal it is the quiet sound of horses munching in a stable at night. The city dweller who has lived all his life amid the hum of urban traffic and the pulsing of machines would never understand. Poor devil!

He has never lived. These things cost nothing, but they are a part of our heritage of life without which we are infinitely the poorer.

It is impossible to explain this fully to anyone who has not experienced these things himself many times. In the same way it is impossible to explain how shooting can be justifiable to a person who is passionately against killing and has never shot. To explain that Nature can be far crueller than Man; to suggest that a good experienced shot, who, in the ordinary course of events should be something of a naturalist and game-preserver, with a good dog, can do more good than harm; to infer that on occasions shooting may take second place to watching and listening; that is all to court disbelief.

All too often emotion and ignorance are the basis of a passionate dislike of shooting against which reasoned argument and logic are unlikely to prevail. It is only when the mists of ignorance and emotion have been dispersed by full understanding and explanation that this dislike can be overcome, at least to a large extent. In this connection the Wildfowler's Association of Great Britain and Ireland is doing a very great deal of good in the propagating of sound views and news on the activities of wildfowlers, both on the question of shooting and in the matter of game-preservation. It is important that the non-shooting public should understand the views of the wildfowler and, for that matter, of the roughshooter also. Formation of a Roughshooters' Association on similar lines would seem to be indicated, for, in a world where the individual is ridden over roughshod, paradoxically the individual must combine with others if he is to retain his rights as an individual.

But we were walking along the shore before dawn listening to the geese. It is in moments such as these that you achieve that feeling of kinship with your dog which is

the true aim of all who shoot with a dog. The common
knowledge that you must tread warily, that the quarry is
close at hand, that the moment of action is not far off,
these are the things that bind man and dog together as
hunters, just as in war a similar hour binds soldiers
together to face a common danger. However, there
should be no fear of bullets unless some remarkably short-
sighted and trigger-happy sportsman arrives on the scene
unexpectedly, which is unlikely at that hour, although it
is unfortunately sometimes a point to bear in mind.

Then comes the moment when the previously recon-
noitred position is found. The hole has been dug, if one is
being used, and it now remains to wait patiently until the
time comes to be ready. That is probably the moment
when consciousness of your surroundings becomes keenest.
Those first moments sitting waiting in silence sharpen the
senses already acute. The smallest sounds are magnified
and the eyes strain to pierce the darkness around. The
cold chill all the while seems to be reaching right inside
the bones, having long penetrated the outer flesh.

Out on the salting, if you are lucky, the birds are talking
to each other. The occasional beat of wings announces
movement. It is possible to identify individual calls.
There was a mallard, there a goose, probably pinkfeet,
that was an oystercatcher, there a curlew, there a red-
shank. Slowly the picture of the birds in front begins to
build up and it is possible to calculate how many there
are likely to be and which way they are likely to fly.

Of course, if it is blowing half a gale and sleeting as
well, very little of this applies, although it may be even
better wildfowling weather. It is certainly best to have
wind, as this does keep the birds down, but like all such
matters it depends on the place and the circumstances.
Even if it may mean that I am in for a poorer bag, I
would rather have clear weather when I can hear the

birds, simply because I like listening to them. The answer is that I am probably not a sufficiently ardent wildfowler to go out in a punt and slither around the mud on my belly.

I like my shooting to have a place for a dog and in a punt there is little or none. The confirmed puntgunner has little use for a dog and, whatever the skills involved, I am personally not greatly attracted to puntgunning as a sport, mainly for that reason. All the same I know of one puntgunner at least who has scrapped his old gun and now goes out round creek and inlet armed with a well choked twelve-bore and accompanied by his dog. He swears he gets just as good bags in this manner and I can well believe that he is right.

However, we were waiting for the dawn and listening to the wildfowl talking and it is surprising how much can be heard even when it is blowing hard. It is surprising, too, how often there is a lull in the weather around dawn. Then rather than midnight is truly the 'witching hour'. As the blackness slowly diminishes so the world begins to waken. First one bird call may be heard then another. Gradually a suspicious whitening appears in the darkness, a tinge of greyness rather than an actual light. Then the first streaks of definite light are there and there is a noticeable lightness in the sky. Then slowly the lightness gives way to colour.

Before the process has gone so far the wildfowler will have heard an upsurge of wings as the congregation of birds in front of him has begun to move as one. A moment later there are birds over him, if he has chosen his place well. Or it may be that all he hears is the whisper of wind in a duck's wings and his only warning is the sharp cocking of his dog's ears. Depending on his position and the weather he may have one shot or he may have twenty. In any event, his shooting is not likely to be a lengthy affair nor his bag a large one. By the time day-light is well on its way his shooting is probably over. Then comes the time to send his dog off to carry out those difficult retrieves. Here is where the wildfowler without a dog is handicapped. How many geese or ducks that would otherwise have been taken home have floated out on an ebbing tide for want of a good dog?

When the last bird has been retrieved the wildfowler can stretch his cramped limbs and look around him at the unfolding glories of another day, or else he can huddle his freezing body inside his bulky clothes and try to keep some of the wetness from soaking down his neck. Then in any case is the moment for the production of the thermos of hot coffee and the flask of whisky. If the sunrise merits watching, the wildfowler may watch it as he fills his pipe or towels his dog dry. He may reflect with scorn, as he watches the cloud formations redden with the rising sun, on the sluggard lie-a-beds who are missing this, or he may trudge homewards wearily wondering if he will ever be dry and warm again and why on earth he came.

In the evening the story is much the same. The wild-fowler takes up his position with his dog as the sun begins to set and prepares for the wildfowl to flight. If he knows his position and can gauge the line of flight correctly he may be able to shoot from one to half a dozen head. Only on exceptional occasions will he be able to claim more. There are of course those rare occasions when the wild-fowler is perfectly placed, when conditions are perfect with strong moonlight and sufficient cloud, when the wildfowl simply keep on coming over throughout the night. Then the bag may be considerably larger. But such occasions are rare indeed. They may fairly be regarded as the just reward of perseverance.

So far I have made no mention of decoys or of stalking or duck ponds and the hundred and one other ways of wildfowling. This is principally because I am writing from the point of view of the man who wants merely to use a twelve-bore and his dog to the full by occasional wildfowling. Admittedly, if a hide is constructed and decoys carefully laid out, a larger bag can be almost assured. If an eight-bore or ten-bore is used birds can obviously be killed at longer ranges. If the birds are shot flighting to specially constructed duck ponds where artificial feeding is laid on, again bigger bags may be anticipated. It is not, however, the size of the bag that should be of primary interest so much as the methods employed in obtaining it.

There is something very special about wildfowling; the momentary glimpse of a dark shadow in the grey sky and the snap shot at the outline of the bird. There is a fascination about that which it is hard to resist. The trouble is that too many people fire impossible shots when the birds are far out of range and spoil the sport for others, as well as merely wounding birds which they do not pick. In the past I have walked round a local foreshore on a Sunday morning with my dogs and they have retrieved as many runners hidden in the coarse grass and reeds, merely tipped in most cases, as I might have expected to shoot. It will be appreciated that this does not in practice mean very many, but goldeneye, teal, wigeon, mallard and even geese are sometimes wounded in this fashion and not retrieved, all for the want of a good dog. Only the thoughtless and ignorant few are responsible for this sort of reckless shooting and every sportsman worthy of the name must deplore it. Unfortunately it has been known to happen. The answer is the Wildfowlers' Club, which can, and to a large extent does, now, control this sort of thing.

In his book *Grey Goose*, Michael Bratby very rightly said: "There can be few sights as displeasing as dead geese in bulk", and I think that goes for most wildfowl.

The fact is, of course, that it does not require a great many geese to make a very large pile. Also, contrary to many people's ideas, it is not a difficult thing to shoot a goose, if it is in range. So many people persist in firing at them when they are at more than double the range.

If anyone can stalk geese and get within twelve-bore range he is performing a very creditable feat. I am not in favour of harrying geese, or any game, come to that, but an honest stalk on wary geese can be a very exciting and instructive expedition. With a well-trained dog crawling belly to the ground behind you, use may be made of stratagem.

Leaving the dog in a position down wind of the geese it is sometimes possible to take advantage of dead ground or cover and move in a half-circle almost upwind of the geese. When a suitable position has been reached as near as can be risked without actively alarming the geese, a sharp call may be given on the 'silent' whistle. The chances are that the dog in his approach directly towards the sound will flush the geese over his handler. I warn anyone who cares to try this, however, that I have only had a very limited number of geese this way myself. It is, however, no blame to the dog if the geese do not move in the required direction. One of the exasperating charms of geese is that they so seldom do fly where you want them.

Even when geese do fly directly over you or in front of you they are very deceptive birds to kill. Like duck their rate of flight is considerably faster than it seems. The novice, to begin with, will certainly miss well behind or below. Even that apparently simple shot at duck flushed from cover on the river bank can result all too often in a clean miss unless due allowance is made. To swing right through and fire well ahead and above is the sound old formula for success.

In practice I like having the geese down with me and

I very seldom interfere with them, so that in a hard winter sometimes several hundreds at a time will come down on my shoot to rest. I pick up the occasional bird that has been shot at long range with a ·22, probably by a farmer protecting his young corn, and there are also the inevitable victims of high-tension wires and similar obstacles, but I do not disturb them unduly. So long as they are not constantly harried I find they will always return and their numbers seem to increase each year.

The same may be said for wildfowl of any sort. Mallard, goldeneye and teal are most common on my stretch of river and, as I only shoot them occasionally and restrict that mainly to the drakes, their numbers increase each year. Mallard especially can be encouraged to stay and breed and the carrion crows, hoodies, and other vermin, predators of their eggs, can be kept clear by the keen roughshooter. In this way, and by actively rearing youngsters, the roughshooter and wildfowler can increase the wildfowl population for the good of all. In the same way the roughshooter aided by his dog can increase the stock of game on his shoot. It is greatly to the credit of the Wildfowler's Association of Great Britain and Ireland that it is putting such facts before an ever wider public, and co-ordinating the efforts of local clubs and individuals.

Both to the roughshooter and wildfowler a good general-purpose dog is always an asset and many shooting memories will be connected with him. Memories of Max include the time when he swam out on an ebb-tide after a mallard with a tipped wing. He had never been down to the foreshore before, yet he swam out into the salt water without hesitation and was soon fifty yards out and heading for Norway. Only after frantic blowings on my whistle and considerable expenditure of breath did I see him to my relief turn back. Admittedly he returned without the bird that time, but it was a game effort for a first

Youngster honours point of older dog by backing.

Early water retrieve. Duck used is encircled with rubber band. It is important to start the youngster off mildly and he should learn to respond to hand signals.

Contrast in style.

attempt. The bird itself was a strong swimmer and diver and I had long lost sight of it in the gathering darkness nor for once did I worry about that. I was only too relieved to have Max back unharmed.

In this connection it is as well for the owner of a game dog to remember not to ask too much of it. There is nothing but thoughtlessness involved in sending the dog on a long heavy retrieve towards the end of a strenuous day. Usually the dog's work can be eased towards the end of the day and no opportunity should be missed of doing so. Nor should the dog be asked to try something that may be dangerous or over-difficult. Especially does this apply in wildfowling. How easy to forget that a flood tide is ripping down an estuary at a deceptive speed. However strong a swimmer, the dog should not be expected to do too much.

If there may be any risk to the dog involved the handler should always regard it as his foremost golden rule that such a risk shall not be incurred. The rule 'Never shoot where you can't see' might have an addition 'Never send your dog where you can't see'. Especially so is this when ice is covering river surfaces. Often the edges are soft and the dog may go through in a place where the owner on the steep bank above it is unable to see or to assist until perhaps it is too late.

Muddy boggy ground should always be carefully examined in the same light. A dog may be just as easily bogged as any other animal, and shifting sand or treacherous bogs have been the death of many dogs before this. So before ordering your dog to retrieve that bird, see where it has landed first. Sometimes it is better to forgo a bird than to risk a dog, for a good dog will go far in his efforts to perform a successful retrieve.

There is one other point of danger to the dog which is all too easily overlooked, simply because it is rarely

L

appreciated until too late. When vermin shooting, the roughshooter may have occasion to shoot a black-backed gull or a cormorant. Either of these birds with their vicious beaks constitute a grave menace to a dog sent to retrieve them unless they are quite dead. A cormorant especially can have an eye out in a moment. This is also a danger to remember when sending the youngster to retrieve wounded carrion or hoodie crows for the first time. It is always worth looking at such matters from the dog's viewpoint and wiser and safer to avoid possible trouble.

Also, once the day is over, need it be said that it is desirable that the handler should look to his dog. Especially is this so if the dog has been swimming in icy water. For the comfort of the dog, as well as the upkeep of the car, it is always worth carrying a towel whenever shooting with a dog. A thorough, brisk rub-down is all that should be required. After that a good bed in his kennel on his return is all he asks. Given that simple attention and care, the danger of an early onset of rheumatism and stiffness is staved off, and he will provide in return many days of unstinting service and pleasure.

FOURTEEN

Two's Company

THE ROUGHSHOOTER, as has been pointed out, like the wildfowler is often a lone sportsman. With his dog and possibly one other companion he is content. He usually does not ask for more. Two's company, three's a crowd, might well be his motto. Yet, although I have stressed that two general-purpose Pointer-Retrievers are not necessarily better than one, there is no doubt that there is a very great attraction in working two dogs together. The sight of the two dogs quartering the ground together and then both freezing into rigid points has a considerable charm of its own. To see each dog quartering the ground independently of the other and to learn from their reactions, the raised head, the pause, the half point, the faint wag of the tail, the lowered head in brief investigation and the continued quartering, are pleasures in themselves. By reading these signs correctly it is possible to tell what has been on the ground you are walking over. It is possible to have warning in advance of what is to come.

Too often, however, when two owners of general-purpose dogs get together for a day's shooting, each of the owners starts apologising in advance.

"My dog isn't used to working with another."

"I use my dog only for retrieving you know, most of the time."

"This is the first time he's been working for some time, of course."

"I don't think he's very reliable out in front."

And so on.

Often all due to the famous saying:

"I just took him out shooting and he worked perfectly."

The day I had with the Colonel was a typical instance of this. He started off at once by proudly showing off his lean and rangy dog which stood as high as a Shetland pony on legs that tapered down to great club feet for all the world like a piece of Jacobean furniture. After I had duly expressed polite appreciation of what good points I could see, he went on from bad to worse.

"Of course I never use him in front you know," he said breezily. "He's a wonderful retriever though. Only snag I find is he's just like a spaniel I once owned. Have to beat him before I start shooting and half-way through the day and then he works perfectly. Otherwise he's a bit wild, you understand."

"I understand perfectly," I agreed.

That I felt was an understatement. The trouble is that you do meet people who treat their dogs like this and there is very little that can be done about it except avoid them like the plague in future. The day followed true to the course I had foreseen as soon as I heard his owner's opening words.

His dog ranged wildly pursued by the Colonel's curses and whistles alike. It rushed through my dog's points and did its best to chase the birds into the next county. It failed to retrieve a hare which was rather too big a mouthful for its snipy jaws and eased its conscience by finishing off what its owner had failed to do cleanly. In fact, all in all, it was a day to be forgotten as fast as possible. Unfortunately it is the sort of deplorable exhibition which is seen only too often. In that it played its part in deciding me to write this book it was probably worth suffering, but it should serve as a warning to those who really think that their dog can train itself without assistance.

Another instance of a slightly different state of affairs was that of Walter's bitch. She was an undersized little thing with an extraordinary long and curly tail and a certain dubiety about her breeding.

"I use her mostly on grouse," he said apologetically. "She's a very good pointer really, but of course I don't use her very often."

To judge by her roly-poly condition this was more than true. However, we went out with the guns for a walk round and it soon transpired that she was a confirmed potterer. Working entirely within gunshot at a steady walk, she was admittedly not without a certain degree of nose. She pointed firmly at a patch of grass and as her owner moved forward to flush the game for her, she dived forward and reappeared with a live rabbit.

"I'm afraid she's not very steady on fur," he said brazenly, as he took it from her with something of a struggle. "But it does save cartridges, you must admit."

"I wouldn't have thought she could move so fast," I answered politely and with perfect truth.

Fortunately her owner seemed impervious to sarcasm and we continued without further incident except that after another half an hour of it I really thought it only fair to the dog to call it a day. Otherwise I felt it might expire with a stroke or something. It was still panting when its owner finally removed it an hour or two later.

To judge by Walter's idea of sport she provided all he wanted. Certainly it was no fault of the dog's that she was as she was. It is always worth reflecting that a man may not be judged by his clothes nearly as infallibly as he may be judged by his dogs. Much can be learned of the owner from the appearance and behaviour of the dog. Especially is this so in the shooting field. Also, frequently there is a resemblance between dog and owner. For instance, as with Walter, a fat and breathless little man

will often own a fat and breathless little dog. All they both
needed was more exercise. But the answer is not always
as simple as that unfortunately.

However, these examples are only one side of the picture. I have had welcome visitors like my old friend
Michael with his well built, promising young dog. That
was a day to remember with pleasure. We had just the two
dogs out. The dogs quartered perfectly, crossing in front of
us and ignoring each other except when one came on
point, when the other honoured it promptly and beautifully.

It was a bad scenting day and with thundery weather
in the offing the game was rather unsettled. However, we
managed to achieve quite a good bag. Three brace of
partridges, two brace of pheasants and six hares in not
much more than four hours' shooting. All that was
pointed was shot and all that was shot was retrieved. But
then Michael is rather a crack-shot. Anyway, that was
certainly a memorable day and the dog-work was not the
least interesting part of it.

In one field of roots especially we had an excellent test
of steadiness. Max came on point to my left and
Michael's dog honoured the point from his side. I then
gave the signal to flush and a cock pheasant was pushed
out which I shot. At this moment, while both dogs were
down, another cock decided to get up on Michael's right.
This one was also decisively downed. We both then gave
the command 'Hie Lost' together. Both dogs moved to
their respective birds and in a few moments both cocks
were in the bag. A highly pleasing and satisfactory
performance.

An interesting point there is that Michael is a good shot
and a good sportsman with sound ideas and his dog
seemed to be shaping in the same way. Conversely I have
noticed the bumptious, loud-mouthed sportsman often

possesses a bumptious, wild and noisy dog. Here is yet another instance of the affinity between dog and master which I mentioned earlier. Often the master's traits are astonishingly reflected in the dog.

This is probably a suitable moment for pointing out that there are occasions, which have not so far been stressed, when the best of dogs makes a mistake. Just as the best of shots occasionally misses an apparently easy shot so now and then the best of dogs may have a lapse. It has already been emphasised that most such occasions are due to the handler ignoring such matters as lack of exercise or signs of indisposition. After all, an animal may have a day or so off colour just like a human being, due to a slight chill or a change of diet or something similar. Whatever the reason there must be times in every handler's memory over which it is best to draw a veil. Very few animals or humans are completely perfect.

A particular occasion when my own face was very red was one day's pheasant shooting. A runner had come down near the keeper's cottage and had run amongst the bushes where the old broody hens had been kept for hatching the eggs and rearing the young pheasants. I sent in Max with a firm 'Hie Lost'.

A moment or two later there was a confused squawking and to my horror he reappeared with an old broody neatly held in his jaws. It was unhurt but the head-keeper wasn't missing a chance like that.

"It'll never lay again," he chuckled, wringing its neck. "That'll be one hen down in the game book."

I still think there must have been some confused goings on under the bushes with a foster-mother defending her offspring, but I know it will be a long time before that particular occasion is allowed to be forgotten. If anyone cares to look it is still recorded in the game book under various, 'One hen'.

Of course with the general-purpose Pointer-Retriever there is one common sin, which, as has been emphasised, correct training should completely avoid. That is, when pointing and holding a hare or rabbit fixed, if the fur leaps literally into the dog's jaws, as can happen, it simply retrieves to hand without a shot being fired. Certain owners, like Walter, merely shrug their shoulders and brazenly say "A cartridge saved." The fact remains that the dog has not been properly trained. A well trained dog will get his nose under the game in any circumstances.

There are, of course, certain other temptations and pitfalls common to all gundogs which it is desirable to avoid. It is not safe for instance to leave a cold and tired dog in the back of a car with shot game after a day's work. There is a danger that, however reliable, the dog will devour the game. Admittedly I have only known this happen once and fortunately not then to one of my dogs, but I have heard of other cases and personally I am not prepared to put it to the test. It is better to keep the game out of harm's way rather than take the risk.

Of course, if the steadiest of dogs is taken out with an unreliable dog and then is set a thoroughly bad example, the owner cannot really blame it if it follows suit. There are few things more annoying or insidious in the shooting field than a dog running wild. The others are almost certain to become unsettled in turn and the sensible thing to do on such occasions is to ask the handler to put his dog on the lead.

It is, however, easy to go on writing about the sins and omissions of owners and dogs on the shooting field. At least the man with a dog of any type is trying to be an all-round shooting man and sportsman, however efficient or inefficient he may be. The loudest critic of any dog's behaviour is usually the man who, when asked where his dog is, replies:

race work on river bank. Pheasant held.

Duck and pheasant shot.

"I haven't got one just now."

Such people when pressed can usually give remarkable accounts of their previous dog's feats of skill and sagacity. If they are to be believed they are usually capable of training anything from a Great Dane to a Peke. They are loud in their denunciations of all breeds of dog other than their own spaniel, labrador, or dalmatian-cross. Dog training to them is just a matter of common sense and careful handling. How right they are.

Whatever breed of dog the true sportsman may own however, he will not care to be unduly dogmatic about it or others. If nothing else, shooting with a dog should very soon teach the handler that he has still a lot to learn both about dogs and about humans. It is easy enough to get led away into descriptions of the ability and prowess of one's own dogs, which would be hard to live up to with a Field Trial Champion. Even if you own a Field Trial Champion, it should never be forgotten that there are always other handlers and other dogs who might be able to perform as well or better should the occasion arise.

In sport, however, especially with dogs, one thing leads to another. This is probably truer with a general-purpose dog than with a specialist dog, for the man who starts off by training one may well end up by training another to keep the first company. There is a satisfaction in watching them work which repetition does not pall nor familiarity stale. There is, of course, the old saying 'Two's company . . .', but it is questionable whether this applies to dogs as it does to men. Naturally the answer must vary, but there is little doubt which the enthusiastic rough-shooter will prefer. Two dogs pointing in unison, two dogs at heel, or two dogs quartering the ground in front, are a sight worth seeing.

FIFTEEN

Extracts from a Training Diary

January 4th.

VILE WEATHER. Sleet and rain. Freezing wind. More wind and colder conditions forecast. Waited three quarters of an hour on station platform for train to arrive with very cold and miserable looking bitch pup on board. Willa, short for Wilhelmina, I presume, is nine months old like Werra and has similar chocolate head and markings though darker liver and white fleckings. Temperament, however, seems entirely different. She is much quieter and less boisterous. However, it is early to judge yet. She seemed very pleased to be off the train and settled down in the car quite comfortably. Also seemed pleased with her new quarters and was ravenously hungry. She does not seem to understand any words of command beyond her name but when she realised what was wanted 'Sat' to command at once. Nothing like starting straight away. It is obvious, however, that she is nothing like as advanced as Werra. It will be interesting to watch how she progresses.

January 5th.

Weather surprisingly improved. Warm and sunny in spite of forecasts to contrary. Initial training begun. Willa taken out on check lead. She walks well to heel on lead and soon picked up idea of sitting to word of command whenever we stopped. She is obviously very intelligent and should not be as much trouble to train as I had feared. Clearly she has plenty of instinct as I note she tends to point at anything strange to her, and judging by the way she uses her nose on everything, that aspect is all right. Am also glad to see that she picks up things in her mouth and carries them about. Retrieving is going to be no bother. I hope.

January 6th.

Weather is still holding well. Am more or less marking time with Werra's training at the moment and am concentrating on Willa. Had her out five times for about a quarter of an hour today and she is coming on amazingly quickly. So far am glad to find that she shows no signs of having been mishandled. She has just not been taught anything at all. However, as she has lived in a town, this is not surprising. I notice she already shows more signs of liveliness and suspect her diet has not been all it might have been. Have started food training as well as work on long lead with raised hand. She sits to command, raised hand, and stamp of the foot already. Is also staying put when I walk away several paces. Comes willingly to command and signal so long as they are accompanied by her name. As yet does not really understand anything but name and 'Sit'. But she is learning very quickly and is easy to teach.

January 8th.

Forecast gloomy. Weather perfect. Willa fully understands 'Sit' and 'Heel' and signals now. Have increased the distance I can walk away to full extent of check lead and she shows no sign of attempting to follow. Will soon be able to take her through full drill without any lead.

January 10th.

Poured with rain yesterday but fine again today. Went through most of primary obedience drill without lead today and Willa behaved perfectly. Have also started her on initial retrieving with small dummy. Threw dummy in full view five yards away and made her sit. Then sent her off after it still on check lead with wave and 'Hie Lost'. She ran forward at once and picked it up. I suspect she would not have returned with it and am almost sure she has played this game before, but by gentle use of lead was able to induce her to return with it. She then sat to command perfectly still with dummy in her mouth while I patted her. She was not keen to give it up which was all to the good. Pressed her lips lightly against her teeth and repeated command 'Dead' and she finally let me have it. Then rewarded her with biscuit. Am not sure this was not a mistake with her as she is definitely greedy. Unlike Werra who eats carefully and slowly Willa wolfs her food. Must remember to take sample of faeces for worm check by vet, though she looks perfectly fit and well. Always worth doing this and I should have done it already.

January 12th.

Weather beginning to break. Getting colder and looks like snow again. Forecast milder warmer weather. How contradictory. Willa's primary obedience progressing well. She is now prepared to sit in front of food and wait while I leave the room. Also stays put to stamp of foot and allows me out of sight for fifteen seconds. Am quite sure time limit can be quickly stepped up with her. She shows no signs of moving now she understands what is wanted. Am having slight trouble with her retrieving as she now drops dummy as soon as she comes forward to sit in front of me. That confounded piece of biscuit was a mistake. However, it should be all right in a day or two. Have simply taken pace or two backwards and encouraged her to pick it up again. This worked but the mistake was repeated on second attempt. My fault not hers.

January 14th.

Still no snow but due any moment by the look of things in spite of forecast of warmer weather. Werra did her first point on wild game today which is big step forward. So far she has merely done near points. This was staunch point on cock pheasant in hedge. When I flushed it I made her sit with command 'Set Up'.

Willa is now progressing very well with her retrieving of small dummy. Goes off at wave of hand and returns with dummy perfectly. Also does all her primary obedience and today introduced her to blank pistol. She showed no sign of alarm and will soon get the idea of dropping to it, I am confident. Should soon be able to take her out with Werra.

January 17th.

Freezing hard and snow all round several inches deep, but forecast ignoring it completely appears to deny its existence. Says warm belt is spreading across Europe. However, training has been going on after a fashion. Willa drops to blank shot very satisfactorily now. Both she and Werra seem to like the snow and have taken them out together for first time today. Made them do elementary primary obedience at first together and then separately. Willa had idea sooner than Werra as she responds to name better. Werra had tendency to respond to any order in spite of not being addressed to her. Shows importance if two dogs are being trained or used together in having them responding to name.

January 20th.

Weather forecast seems to have woken up to fact that snow is lying everywhere and gloomily prophesies more yet. The training thus is somewhat spasmodic and have been concentrating on fast walks round large shed to persuade Werra to keep perfect position at heel. Seems to be having desired effect. Am also improving both their quartering and ranging. Willa is inclined to be a little timid about wandering far from me whereas Werra is always inclined to roam too far. Hence am not overdoing heel training for Willa and I hope their ranging together will help to improve their faults. It seems to be working all right so far but obviously not a good plan to overdo this as they have a tendency to follow each other.

January 22nd.

Weather forecast should have stuck to its guns. Thaw set in abruptly and ground is soaking wet. However, was able to get in some more training and had Willa on more advanced retrieving with larger dummy. Went through entire primary obedience drill including dropping to blank shot and she is getting the idea splendidly. Introduced gun and put it up to shoulder over her head, having dropped her, and then kept putting it up and brandishing it suitably at intervals. She was really alarmed at first. I suspect she may have been threatened with a stick at some time. Am convinced if she had been shot over without preparation she would have become gun-nervous. Am quite sure this is the case with most so-called gun-shy dogs. Was discussing this with Michael the other day and he said he had once cured a gun-shy dog by tying it up and firing shots over its head in a 'kill or cure' attempt. Really gun-shy hysterical dog would have probably had a fit. I do not believe there is any cure for really gun-shy dogs and they should never be bred from or used as anything but pets.

January 21st.

Went out with gun again and Willa much less shy of it today. Still is inclined to leap sideways if I swing it over her head suddenly when she is walking at heel. Will soon be over this, however, and will then be able to graduate to shots fired. Meanwhile she is retrieving well and fetches dummy from long stubble and similar places with a wave of hand. She has every bit as good a nose as Werra. It will be interesting to watch her pointing and following laid trail.

January 25th.

Relapse in weather which according to forecast should have been mild has interrupted things but primary obedience is really sound now and it only remains to bring Willa on to rolled turnips. The old croquet ball seems to have been mislaid temporarily. I expect it will turn up in the way things do. Anyway turnips and suitable logs of wood are quite good enough. Have the advantage they can be fired at without any damage. Once she is over that and has started pointing she will be nearly up with Werra who is now pointing quite regularly and goes down whenever anything is flushed. Have not, however, started her on flushing of her own accord yet.

January 26th.

Mild and sunny weather which was actually forecast correctly for once. Willa was tested on rolling dummy today for the first time. Had her on check lead which she resented but just as well as she showed inclination to run in after it. Was checked with sharp tug and warning 'No' and looked suitably ashamed. Did one repeat on lead and then tried her free. She was as good as gold for that and several repeats so then I tried it on her when she was ranging freely and not expecting it, also firing a blank at same time. Am glad to say it worked well though I felt I was forcing the pace a little. The snag is that with many interruptions with the weather one is more or less forced to push on ahead while one can. At least it is a great temptation though one must try to avoid it. However, no harm done as it turned out.

January 29th.

Big step forward today. Introduced Willa to shot. First in distance and then with her behind. Was pleased to find I had judged it correctly and she took no more notice than if it had been the blank after her first slightly puzzled look at the noise. She now is absolutely sound on primary obedience and drops to the rolled dummy and shot. At same time has taken first steps in retrieving. So is now ready for pointing. As partridges are now pairing this should be easy enough.

January 31st.

Took Willa out on check lead and quartered her gently towards spot where I knew partridges were lying. Check lead rather disconcerted her at first but I saw her head go up almost at once as she scented partridges. Held her rigid then and checked her tendency to draw on by standing quite still myself. After half a minute firmly held I advanced cautiously up to her holding her still and by this time she was staunch and trembling with excitement. Soothed her down all over from head to tail and made much of her. Then flushed the birds with loud 'Set Up' and pleased to find she went down at once. Have once or twice on quartering recently noticed her tendency to rush up on a scent and I thought the check lead advisable but am reasonably sure now that we won't need it again. She remained staunch for a full minute at least. Once that has happened it is not usually necessary to use the check lead again unless for flushing. What we now require is a nice fat hare firmly ensconced in its form and we can start them on flushing. Werra, I think, already has the idea as she moved on a cock pheasant yesterday afternoon without any attempt at mouthing, having done a perfect point in the first place. It is now becoming quite exciting taking them out. Will soon be interesting to see them out together and get them backing each other. At the moment, however, keeping them separate.

February 1st.

Might have known the weather couldn't hold in spite of favourable forecasts. More snow. Very tiresome just at interesting stage in training. Reduced to quartering and walking to heel and primary obedience training.

February 4th.

Signs of a thaw bringing with it rain. Forecast a general freeze-up which would be tiresome.

February 6th.

First day suitable for training proper even if it is Sunday. Snow gone again although it will probably return soon by the feel of the wind. Glad to find that both dogs were sound on their points. Willa taken on flushing was encouraged to move on rabbit which seemed to imagine it was invisible in stubble. She made a half hearted attempt to get it in her mouth after being urged forward with command 'Set Up'. Was checked at once with fierce 'No'. Am pleased to record that she thereupon dropped it at once and allowed it to run past her nose in most tantalising fashion. Am sure if she had been trained on a stuffed rabbit skin she would have seized it automatically. That I think is responsible for most of these initial mouthings. Anyway after that she performed perfectly on an old buck hare about as large as herself who looked at her contemptuously before loping off with a hitch of his hindquarters and a couple of half hops. Werra has by this time got the drill perfectly and so I think the time has come to press to on retrieving proper.

February 8th.

Saw the sun for the first time for what seems weeks. Used old Khaki Campbell drake as dummy and began

M

advanced retrieving lessons. Used a piece of old inner tubing round body holding wings and head in and tried him out once on each puppy. Glad to say that training must have been sound because both took to him quite happily. Still perfectly serviceable for roasting, though a bit tough. Annoying that it is now close season as will have to lay trails with rabbits which is never so satisfactory. However, first of all have stepped up dummy training and having dummies thrown around puppies as they retrieve and shots fired. From now on an assistant is absolutely necessary the whole time really, which is sometimes a little tiresome. Also had both out together today for first time. Both froze rigidly on point at a smell. Don't know for certain what it was but suspect wily old cock pheasant. Both looked very perturbed at being mistaken and also looked accusingly at each other as if to lay blame elsewhere. After that Werra had first point on hare and Willa came on from the other side a moment later. Quite good for a start. Both went down on my flushing it.

February 10th.

Certain amount of kennel jealousy to contend with but I think it will soon settle down. Werra refuses to honour Willa though Willa duly honours her. Willa more mild of two personalities and suspect Werra is using form of psychological warfare on her. I think with perseverance it will come out all right but can see it is going to be tiresome for a little.

February 12th.

Weather is still unsettled in spite of persistent reports of sunshine everywhere else. However managed to lay two trails today. Had to use a rabbit which was rather tiresome as I much prefer partridge or bird for this initial practice. However both performed quite pleasingly. Werra was a little uppish after finding hers and gave

rabbit a mild shake. Cautioned her at once with a firm
'No' and then made much of her when she returned it to
hand. It is difficult to say but I think she moved a little
faster on the scent though was possibly a little more
careless than Willa which is perfectly in keeping with the
difference in their characters. How anyone can say that
all dogs are alike I do not know. As well say all Chinamen,
Englishmen. Scots and Arabs are alike. All are men.

February 14th.

Sunshine seems to have returned. Was pleased to find
that kennel jealousy seems to have disappeared as suddenly as it developed. Both puppies were quartering well
and each did one perfect point which was honoured by the
other. Each went down correctly and time has nearly
come when they could be shot over. At first they will have
to be taken separately but very soon, once they have idea
of the thing, they will be working together. There are
still some ragged points. Their quartering is in need of
improvement. Have not yet had them in water as it is
still too cold by far to start them off though Werra, I
know, would be all right as she goes in of her own accord
whenever she gets the chance. They are both prepared to
face thick cover now. Have not yet, however, had them
hunting in cover. Awkward time of year to train the
young puppies really.

February 16th.

First time either of them actually had game killed over
them. Took them out in turn and made them walk to
heel while I shot pigeon. Am glad to say training proved
adequate in each case, and no attempt was made to run
in even when I stamped foot and went on ahead to
collect pigeons myself. Willa's training especially has been
very gratifying. It shows what can be done with a puppy
full of instinct and intensive training. On the whole

though, would never recommend taking it so fast unless it was specially desired to do so, as in this case to catch up with Werra. Interesting to note that Willa's worst feature was handling of gun over her head. With Werra it was retrieving to hand. Am sure someone must have scolded or smacked the latter at some time for running off with something. However, each is now at stage where their training may continue with the gun in the field. I have a feeling of satisfaction every time I watch them out together and I am looking forward to using them in the field in earnest. Must always bear in mind, however, my own favourite saying that training of dog and man is never over. There is always something fresh to learn.

SIXTEEN

Diary of an Ex-Policewoman

WHEN FREDRIKA II came to me from the Metropolitan Police Training Establishment where her mother Fredrika I had been justly famed for her feats of tracking I was warned that she was eighteen months old and a 'case' and probably gunshy. This is the diary of her training.

Saturday 15th December

I met my wife and Fredrika II off London train. Both were somewhat distrait. F.II had been in such a nervous condition that every noise of the train had caused her to stand on her head behind my wife's back to the detriment of her suit. Feelings were strained. It was fortunate, however, that they were able to travel together, as I hate to think what would have happened if F.II had been travelling in the luggage van alone. She is a complete bundle of nerves. I have never seen a grown dog so flabby, fat and out of condition. She looks as if she is in pup. Her pads are as soft as young pups. Obviously she has had no real exercise for some time and has at the same time been too well fed on a rich Metropolitan Police diet of steaks and sirloins. The slightest noise such as striking a match is liable to send her literally up the wall, or else round in frantic circles to find a place to hide her head. She looks like being a problem. However I had no time this evening to do more than feed her a small meal and let her get settled in the kennel. I will take her out tomorrow and see if we can find a suspected cock runner left from today's covert shooting.

Sunday 16th December

Poor old F. I took her out gently over the fields and had to lift her over walls and ditches as she is far too fat and out of condition to cope with them. She obviously did not know how to begin to do so. Having clapped my hands at her I noticed that she tried to run away the first time and then looked up to see what it was all about. I did not believe she was really gun shy; just gun nervous and everything else nervous. When we reached the area where the cock had been marked Werra came on point almost at once. The cock was flushed on order. I fired a shot at it, watching F., and missed. F. took off and disappeared. Knowing she could not jump a fence, or wall, I went in search of her and found her at last, wandering round vaguely. Meanwhile Werra returned with the cock, which she had retrieved without assistance from me. In the afternoon I took F. out on check lead and fired another shot, to which she did not object unduly. Undoubtedly she is only gun nervous. But very out of condition. It will be a six months' job just to get her fit.

Monday 17th December

In the late afternoon I took the dogs out and concentrated on trying to get F. to sit to command. She ran away, but Werra joined in and showed her how. Very primly. On the check lead she behaves perfectly, but off it she behaves just as she pleases. I did not fire a shot, as I only saw one pigeon in the darkening, but, all the same, I am sure she is much happier already. She is a clear case of arrested development, due to always having been in a kennel and never having been seriously taught anything at all, or having had anyone really taking a personal interest in her. She loathes anything flapping, e.g. washing on the line. She still starts at the slight noises, if unexpected, but is already better than she was. She obviously needs some home life and fun and games. She will probably retrieve all right, as the first thing she did on seeing hens was to run in and seize one. She gripped it by the neck and would not bring it to me. She ran off determinedly and I had to get her cornered, hold her, and give her a few strokes with the check lead while holding the fluttering hen in front of her. Fortunately the hen was quite unhurt. I think this treatment may have cured her, but hope it doesn't affect her retrieving. I only want to stop her chasing hens. We can't have that, but it doesn't seem to have worried her.

I am certain that she is putting on this neurotic appearance as she enjoyed mock retrieving with the dummy in the house; running back to her basket and being intercepted before she could chew it. I am cutting down her food to try and get her waistline back. She is disgustingly fat and out of condition. However, she may make a gundog yet. The mistake I made today was to have her on the check lead beside me. Once off it she tried to stay to heel consistently and refused to roam. She is probably easily tired, but this could very quickly become a bad habit and I must get her out hunting. I will have to risk letting her run in and chase in order to get some more original bitch in her. This is clearly a case where orthodox measures would be useless.

Tuesday 18th December
I took the three dogs out in quest of a hare and a rabbit. Almost at once we flushed a hare downwind in the grass field below the hill. Fredrika was with me and ran in after it. I shot it cleanly before she could get near it with

her ridiculous waddle. Max retrieved it and she made an
abortive nibble at it as he brought it back. In the next
field Werra drew on well on a trio of partridges, running
ahead. I took one stone dead and she retrieved well to
order. After some more wanderings in growing darkness
I fired two abortive barrels at a rabbit, which Werra
pointed well, but which Fredrika spoiled by running in
through the point. The rabbit lives to run another day.
If it is the same one I have persecuted this season in that
drain I must have now fired at it at least seven or eight
times. What a confession. Its pants must be almost armour
plated by now.

The verdict on Fredrika is that she is certainly not
gunshy. She embraced my leg and leaped up after most
shots to seek reassurance, but gave that up latterly and
the run-in after the hare and the rabbit probably did her
some good, though both were quite abortive as she is too
fat to do much. However I left her to climb over walls
and through fences as best as she could and she is slowly
learning her way about. At present with that absurd
weight to carry she is so soft she can't hope to jump much
and her pads are obviously itching a lot after the unaccus-
tomed stubble. She is also tired out. The answer is that
for a neurotic bitch work is the remedy. Psychologists in
Harley Street would no doubt often like to prescribe the
same thing. She is no longer gunshy and is far less nervous.
She is sleeping well in spite of noise. She is showing signs
of house training as she is a naturally clean dog.

She may be difficult to teach to retrieve and she shows
no sign of pointing at all yet, but that and the hunting
instinct ought to come fairly soon. She might have quite
a gentle mouth·if she can be stopped from chewing. At
the moment she chews anything and everything just like a
teething pup. She certainly ought to point easily enough.
She uses her nose a lot but has a cold which can't help.

At the moment I am concentrating on getting her to sit when told. Basic obedience must come first. After she is fully obedient to the command 'Sit' I will go on. If she builds up muscle and is kept hungry she should work all the more willingly for a few bribes. On the whole I feel she might make a gundog yet and am certainly not in despair. It might be a very long job as she is slow to learn, but she does try to help and co-operate and, being conscious of her antecedents, one can't blame her unduly. She might turn out surprisingly well, once she is fully developed mentally and physically.

She must learn to obey at a distance first above all. Today I did my best at intervals to rub this in and feel she would have tried to keep up with the others, but she was so tired that she stuck close to heel most of the time and was even underfoot in an annoying fashion. She looked quite hurt when I tried to move her on. However she has essentially an easy and helpful nature, I feel, under her neurosis and flabbiness.

Wednesday 19th December
I shot a hare going steeply uphill in front of Fredrika. It got up at her feet and rolled back in full view of her nerve kicking, although stone dead. She half stiffened into a point as she watched it. Werra also sat watching it roll back past her. Good training for both of them.

Friday 21st December
We walked round the foot of the hill. Werra came on point at the fence and Fredrika lumbered up, still unmuscled, and came on her first near point at the sight of Werra. Tail out, body straight and leg up, backing for about five seconds. At least this proves the instinct is there. She is still gamely trying to follow the others and does seem to be coming on quite rapidly, all things

N

considered. She is not in the least frightened now really. At least compared with her immediate arrival. I did not shoot all day, but tested her in the shallow water by the islands. She did show signs of fright at first, but came on, after encouragement, and waded belly deep quite cheerfully. Yesterday she fell in up to the waist, but today was quite deliberate and after her first misery she took to it quite cheerfully. She has longer hair than the other two, but seemed to dry off quite well.

Monday 24th December

Fredrika is beginning to learn. She lacks confidence and strength, but shows instinct and willingness. She will be slow, but may well turn out very good in the end. Although she has had no real retrieve, or point, yet she shows more interest.

Wednesday 3rd January

I walked round the hill with William and the three dogs. Werra well in front moved a hare back behind her. I gave it both barrels, but regret to say only wounded it. Fredrika ran in and turned the hare back to Max, who was sitting waiting beneath hill and simply had to open jaws to receive it. Fredrika then ran downhill and seized it from him and brought it to me. Her first retrieve on game. All wrong, but better than nothing. Beyond the wood William rolled over a hare in front and Fredrika ran in and seized it firmly and retrieved it well. Between us in the wood we shot one cock and one hen which Fredrika retrieved.

Fredrika retrieved two more hares and we shot another cock. Ten head in all. Quite a pleasant day, if nothing spectacular. Verdict on Fredrika is that she is going to be all right. She must learn to drop when told, or it will be hopeless, but this will come. She was running in madly today, which is at least an improvement on her tameness and lack of initiative of the past. She has begun to wake up and can retrieve quite well. She should settle down and will, I think, be naturally soft-mouthed in spite of this beginning.

Friday 5th January
Fredrika did a very poor retrieve on a hare in the plough. She still has not strength enough to carry them over rough going.

Monday 8th January
Fredrika, who obstinately refused to pick the dummy earlier today, went and retrieved a hare on a blind retrieve in gorse and did it very well. She has a phobia about the dummy and I suspect the police tried to make her pick it and she now has a reaction to it. I will have to take her gently, or could ruin her now. She picked a hare later on today, but would not bring it to hand. Must not force the pace unduly. All her training will have to be at her speed and as the needs of the moment indicate, as she is too old to train on normal lines. She backed Werra well on point, but so far has not had a genuine point of her own. All the time however her instincts are growing stronger. She should be good one day.

Tuesday 9th January
We walked round the boundaries towards hill. Fredrika had a point of her own and, when I did not immediately follow it up, flushed a hen pheasant. A pity I was not up with her. It was a good point. Max then flushed a cock pheasant out of the wood unexpectedly over my shoulder. I took a snap shot at long range and saw it plane down. On a hunch I followed it up and Werra came on point. Then she flushed the cock over river and I made no mistake this time. It landed stone dead on the far bank. I sent Max into the water and he leaped in eagerly. After

a second's hesitation Fredrika followed him and by the time he reached the bird it was neck and neck. Fortunately she did not try to seize the bird, but followed him back with every sign of wishing to do so. In a way would have been interesting to see if she would have retrieved it. She would obviously retrieve from water itself, which is most illuminating as she is distinctly showing signs of being difficult about retrieving now. Perhaps I have been pushing her too hard. She has obviously been mishandled with a dummy at some time and quivers with fright when asked to retrieve it, or rather when it is put in her mouth, as she will not even pick it up now. This is silly as a few days ago she was willing to fetch it after a fashion. However she is now in season and this may not be helping much. Probably it is partly that.

I can see why the police got tired of her. She can be quite infuriating. I must be careful not to handle her roughly in any way however, although the temptation is very great when she acts, and that is the operative word, stupid on a subject she is known to understand perfectly well. This is a real test of patience. Everything else is easy compared to trying to teach something to an animal apparently scared of lessons. The mind seems to be gripped by the fear of some happening in the past and nothing functions at all, although quite a good mind in practice. The answer with her at the moment would appear to be to leave dummy training well alone and concentrate on giving her plenty of outside retrieving and work. She did a second point of her own today, on a hole. It was confirmed by Werra. Presumably a rabbit. Later on she did some nice backing. Only the retrieving appears to be suffering at the moment.

Wednesday 10th January
Fredrika mouthed a partridge, but did not retrieve it.

No real damage done fortunately, either to the partridge or her. I hope.

Thursday 11th January

Fredrika is now definitely much fitter. She careered away after a hare and retrieved an old mangy specimen of rabbit to hand, after mouthing it. She is muscling up now and beginning to get at least some idea of being a gundog.

Friday 12th January

On the hilltop we moved a hare which Fredrika promptly chased. From my position above her I bowled it over cleanly and Fredrika retrieved it to hand well. Not too bad considering that earlier today she refused to fetch the dummy at all. She is obviously windy of any training, but enjoys work. She set off after another hare. The time is approaching for use of check cord.

Sunday 14th January

Today Fredrika twice ran in and seized a rabbit from Werra and brought them to hand after mouthing. Yet this evening she would not retrieve on dummy at all. Nor unfortunately will she run in on the check cord as she feels she is on the lead. Altogether a difficult animal. However this was more or less what was expected. She just is not behaving in the same way twice running, so that it is difficult to work out any reasons for her actions and work out counters.

Tuesday 16th January

Today I decided Fredrika is merely putting on a neurotic act. She will not retrieve the dummy and I feel the time has come when drastic methods must be applied, since nothing else appears to work.

Wednesday 17th January

I started today by tying the dummy in F.'s jaws. A couple
of pieces of string were tied round the dummy and joined
behind her head. Then I put her on the check lead and
led her round for ten minutes. To begin with she was the
picture of misery, shivering with fear, mostly pretence,
and could not have looked more abject. After five minutes
she cheered up and after ten minutes she was walking
happily beside me, wagging her tail. She would sit and
come with it when called. I untied the dummy and she
still retrieved perfectly with no attempt at mouthing. In
the afternoon I shot a hare and she ran in and mouthed
badly and would not retrieve. What a dog, I must be
forcing the pace too hard. One thing at a time. The dummy first and check cord to stop her running in next. I only
hope I can get her to run in with it on and bowl her over.
She should not need it more than once.

Friday 19th January

Today I tied the dummy in Fredrika's mouth once more.
Again it worked perfectly and she carried it without
strings for a short period before delivering to hand without mouthing.

Saturday 20th January

The previous training has now paid off. She is now
carrying the dummy well, without attempting to mouth,
or make any protest. The next stage is getting her to pick it
up and retrieve it. She is very close to this, but I must not
make the mistake of forcing the pace. She ran in after a
hare and disappeared over the hill. She came back dead
lame and suspect a greenstick fracture. Perhaps this will
teach her. But I doubt it. I will now have to take her
gently for a week or so.

Sunday 28th January

She is now retrieving the dummy perfectly without hesitation and enjoying doing so. There is no attempt at mouthing. This makes training much easier. Although her leg is now better she is showing less sign of wanting to run in, so perhaps she did learn something after all.

Friday 2nd February

I laid a trail for Fredrika today, which she followed quite well and retrieved the hare at the end of it extremely well. She is now coming on in leaps and bounds.

Saturday 3rd February

I spoke too soon. Fredrika reverted to mouthing. She made a complete nonsense of the retrieve of a hare. Better to draw a veil over today.

Sunday 4th February

Fredrika is now pointing very well. She is extremely stylish and obviously has a very good nose. The only thing she lacks here is experience. If I can now get her retrieving really well and get her completely steady she will be likely to make a really good dog.

Wednesday 28th February

Fredrika caught and ate a rabbit while I was laying traps today. I made her retrieve the hind legs, which were all that was left. She did this perfectly without mouthing. Then refused to retrieve another she had pointed, which I shot. However I put it down and made Werra mark it and retrieve it in full view of Fredrika. Then she did the same perfectly. It is surprising what a little example, combined with jealousy, can do. She still bumbles about a lot, instead of quartering well, but she has come on really remarkably well considering the mess she was. She points very well and backs excellently and her retrieving is coming on very reasonably. Also she is a lot steadier.

Sunday 11th March

Fredrika retrieved a jay well. She is now retrieving anything to order, with the minimum of mouthing. In fact she has a gentle mouth as I always suspected and does try to please. She is now almost reliably steady, although full of life and go.

Sunday 18th March

I took F. out alone. She quartered reasonably, if erratically. She pointed two rabbits, which were shot over her and both retrieved on order, without attempt to run in. She can be said to be partially trained now.

Tuesday 20th March

Fredrika retrieved a crow very well indeed. She is now beginning to be reliable and only needs to improve her quartering.

Friday 20th April

Fred put up her last black today. I hope. She chased a sheep in the field. I took her straight off to a pen where the old rams were being held and let them butt her unmercifully. I doubt if she will ever look at a sheep again.

*   *   *

The following month she entered her first Field Trial. She was taken down to London by car and, perforce, spent most of the day there without exercise. The following morning, rising at five-thirty, I gave her a two hour run in the country, when she began to show signs of waking up a little, but barely answered the whistle to start with at all. With some misgivings I took her to the

Field Trial. In the morning she ran very badly, but there was little game for her to point. In fact she neither saw nor missed any, but quartered very badly. In the afternoon she woke up in the second stake and quartered very well indeed, but again had no game to point. Hence she was put down. However she was the only dog to succeed in what was described by the judge as 'a difficult retrieve for the very best dog one might think of'. She did it twice without undue encouragement, whereas only one other dog succeeded in performing it at all and then only after some time had elapsed. On the whole it was a very pleasing performance for a first effort.

Friday 29th June
Fred and I were out together. She pointed seven rabbits in succession, which were each bowled over and then retrieved, on order, to hand. I also shot a pigeon, which she marked and retrieved to hand perfectly. I reckon she could now be said to be a useful working dog.

Sunday 5th August
Fredrika ran second to Werra in the Novice Stakes of the Scottish Field Trials Association Setter and Pointer Trial. She had two very long range points indeed and drew up on them very well. In her first run she came on point and the young dog running against her stole the point, but she backed perfectly. In the afternoon she had a point and drew on for some hundred and fifty yards, or more, very steadily, before finally flushing a covey. I feel she has been very well worth all the trouble involved.

SEVENTEEN

Postword. Mainly on the G.S.P.

I HAVE so far deliberately avoided making special reference to any particular breed of gundog. This is largely because I have seen roughshooters with excellent general-purpose dogs of almost every breed and description and because when shooting the choice in all matters of gun, cartridges, equipment, companions and dog, must be a purely personal one. Also, although almost any breed of gundog can be trained in this way, there are many recognised breeds of general-purpose dog and it is invidious to make comparisons. There are good and bad in every breed and like everything else there are fashions in these matters, which, as fashions will, alter from time to time.

A good instance of this latter point is the present lapse from favour of the Gordon Setter. This very useful breed used to do, and no doubt still can do, all that has been described in this book and was one of the most popular breeds in Germany for this reason, prior to the turn of the century. It was only then slowly superseded by the German Shorthaired Pointer (G.S.P.), which had been growing in popularity there since the breed records were begun in 1871.

For the past seven years, as the illustrations in this book will indicate, I have personally inclined towards the G.S.P. because I have found it would readily do all that

I required and more. Since there has been a considerable interest shown in the breed and a certain amount of misunderstanding about them, I feel it might be worth making some points clear. To begin with, therefore, a brief history of how the breed was originally developed and an indication of the purposes they were used for will help to explain their instinctive understanding of what is required from the general-purpose dog.

The breed results from careful crossing of the old Spanish Pointer with the German Schweisshund, or bloodhound, and the indigenous Shorthair stock. The cross was finally stabilised in the 1870s and was then bred for nose, speed, power and endurance sufficient to contend with large game such as deer and wild boar. As an all-purpose dog they were expected to track down and retrieve anything from fox and wildcat to pheasant, partridge, woodcock and hare. They proved a complete success both at pointing and retrieving, being extremely intelligent, biddable and tough.

The arguments advanced against them by their critics in this country were that they must be hard-mouthed because they were sometimes trained in Germany to finish off their game. Similarly it was argued that they were expected to do too much and that if they were to trail wounded game for considerable distances they could not still be sound pointers or air scenters. The answer is that bred and trained in this country as we train a retriever, they should and do have as gentle a mouth as any gundog and, since we do not expect them to do undue tracking or foot-scenting, the latter argument is not tenable.

It is too much to expect everything from one dog. If the dog has previously been trained to hunt roe deer, and to spring in eagerly to the fall, it must follow that different standards of what is soft-mouthed·must prevail.

Some people will always argue that rat killing does not necessarily make their retriever hard-mouthed and unreliable on feather, but it seems to me that if you are after roe deer and you collect a slightly damaged pheasant as well you haven't got a great deal to complain about. With a dog of some generations breeding and training as a gundog in this country, as we train our dogs, the question should not arise.

Surprisingly enough, one thing that has caused a certain amount of opposition to the breed in this country has been the docked tail. This is due to misleading comparisons with the English Pointer. It must be remembered that the G.S.P. is a quite separate and distinct breed of Pointer-Retriever. It is expected to work in cover as well as the open. Anyone who has seen an undocked tail bleeding after work in rough cover will appreciate the reason for docking. It would be as unreasonable to compare a Spaniel with an English Pointer and to object because their tails are also docked.

A point of interest about the breed is that they seem generally to show extremely early development of instinct. They may well be pointing instinctively from a very early age and they will very frequently be making attempts to retrieve, by picking up articles and carrying them around, from the moment they are weaned. On the other hand they are usually also extremely late physical developers; most of the breed not having reached full physical development before two years of age or more. There is, therefore, a very great temptation to work the youngster beyond its powers too soon, thereby spoiling its work.

I have personally not found any hardness of mouth with the G.S.Ps. I have handled and seen. The most gratifying things I have found with them as a breed are their willingness to please and their readiness to adapt themselves to their handler's wishes as well as their extreme hardiness and stamina. It is easy to repeat stories of sagacity and resource, but it has always been my feeling that owners are too easily prepared to let enthusiasm get the better of their judgement in this way. In fact, undue boosting without adequate substantiation of their very sound claims in the field has been responsible for a good deal of the scepticism concerning this breed. That is perfectly understandable.

Whatever breed of dog the roughshooter may own, he will always find that it pays to set a high standard in training. Nor should he be readily discouraged if at first results do not seem to be as satisfactory as he would wish. It has been stressed that no dog or handler is ever likely to reach perfection. On the other hand, once a measure of success has been achieved, both dog and handler should experience a feeling of mutual satisfaction in their work which more than repays the effort involved. Each should then go on, as part of a team, learning from the other and achieving an increasingly higher standard.

With a gun and a game bag, the roughshooter and his dog can then go hunting in the truest sense of the word. There is no need for the dog to give tongue. Working mute, he still passes his message to his handler. Whatever may be the quarry, whether it be hare shooting, or, at the opposite end of the scale, snipe, the roughshooter is hunting no less than if he had a full pack of hounds at his command.

Whatever may be the day therefore, whatever may be the method employed, whether there be several guns and several dogs, or merely one man and one dog, the same message holds good.

"Good hunting."

SHORT GLOSSARY OF TECHNICAL TERMS

Quartering	An efficient method of hunting the ground combining the maximum use of nose and gamefinding qualities.
Bracework	Two dogs working in unison. Method depends on ground.
Marking (Fall of Game)	Watching and memorising where birds fall.
Heel Scent	The scent track leading away from the game.
Cheeper	Young game bird.
Clean pick up	Game retrieved steadily without mouthing or excitement.
Clean delivery	Game delivered to hand without mouthing or excitement.
The long drop	To drop at a distance from handler on command.
To hold game	To keep game fixed by staunch pointing.
To back	To honour the point of another dog on sight.
To draw on	To advance steadily on point towards game.
To acknowledge flush	To drop to flushed game.
To road out	To work out scent to ensure all game has gone once flushed.
False pointing	Pointing where no game lies.
False backing (Old term)	Passing another dog on point.
Blinking (Old term)	Can mean not remaining staunch on point. Returning to handler. Can also mean failing to point game.
Break field	To enter in front of handler.
Pottering	Lacking pace and failing to cover the ground adequately. Usually due to lack of 'nose'.
Hoe	Old command for steadying dog on point. Corruption of Toho, in itself corruption of Soho used in hare coursing. Derived directly from Sohowe a term of encouragement to hounds when picking up a line.